All-New Fire HD 8 & 10 User Guide Newbie to Expert in 2 Hours!

by Tom Edwards & Jenna Edwards

Other Books By Tom & Jenna Edwards

250+ Best Fire and Fire HD Apps for the New Fire Owner Amazon Echo User Guide: Newbie to Expert in 1 Hour!

Amazon Echo User Guide - Newbie to Expert in 1 Hour!

Amazon Echo Show User Guide - Newbie to Expert in 1 Hour!

Amazon Echo Dot User Guide - Newbie to Expert in 1 Hour!

Amazon Alexa User Guide - Newbie to Expert in 1 Hour!

All-New Fire 7 User Guide: Newbie to Expert in 2 Hours

Before We Start – Important!

Throughout this book we recommend certain webpages that might be useful to you as a Fire tablet owner and user.

A lot of the webpages we recommend are on Amazon, and a typical Amazon web address might look something like this:

http://www.amazon.com/dp/B00DBYBNEE?encoding=UTF8&camp=1789&creative=9325&linkCode=pf4&linkId=UPTTB3CK67NSPERY&primeCampaignId=prime_assoc_ft

The link above takes you to the Amazon Prime sign-up page, but that's a lot of characters for you to type! So for the longer links we've used what they call a Link Prettifier to make the links shorter and easier to use.

In this example the shortened link is – **amzn.to/2JHgyoN** – if you type that into your browser, it will save you lots of typing time, but still take you straight to Amazon Prime....

Contents

INTRODUCTION

Welcome

When we first published our Fire tablet App review guide - 250+ Best Kindle Fire and Fire HD Apps for the New Kindle Fire Owner - we added in a small bonus section which included a few tips and tricks for the new Fire tablet user.

We soon started receiving emails from customers asking for more of the same, so we published the first Kindle Fire User Guide in 2013.

Since then Amazon have continued to upgrade both their Fire tablet hardware and operating system and each time we have updated our guides to reflect the latest new features.

So, what you hold in your hands today is, our complete and comprehensive, easy to understand guide to getting the most from the all new HD 8 and HD 10 Fire tablets.

We've taken everything we know, scoured the official online Amazon guides, then read a whole lot more and put it all together for you here. What you are reading now is a user guide for both beginners and the tech savvy.

This book contains the basics you need to navigate easily around your device but also the more advanced tips and tricks that will have you using your Fire tablet like a pro before you know it.

How to Use This Book

Feel free to dip in and out of different chapters, but we would suggest reading this Fire tablet owner's manual from start to finish to get a clear overview of all the information contained. We have purposely kept this Fire tablet tutorial short, sweet and to the point so that you can consume it in a couple of hours and get straight on with enjoying your new Fire HD8 or HD10 tablet.

This book is a Fire HD manual specifically concerned with the latest Fire HD 8 tablet released in 2020 and the HD 10 tablet released in October 2017.

The topics we cover include...

- A general Fire tablets review

- Fire HD 8 & HD 10 Specs

- Fire tablet setup instructions

- Fire tablet storage

- Best apps for the Fire HD tablets

- Fire tablet family features

- How to download Fire tablet games, including Underground apps & games

- How to enjoy Fire tablet music and films

We also cover Fire tablet features like

- Fire tablet second screen feature

- Fire tablet mirroring feature

- Fire tablet Amazon Kids (formerly FreeTime) app for kids

- The new Fire tablet microSD card and slot

- Fire tablet Bluetooth pairing

- Fire tablet Text to Speech

- Amazon Cloud Drive and Cloud Collections

- Word Runner & Word Wise

- On Deck for Films & TV

If you have any other questions you can email us **BestKindleApps@gmail.com** but this Fire HD operation manual also has links to

- Fire Tablet HD Customer Services

- Fire Tablet HD Help videos

- Fire Tablet Quick Start Guide

- Fire Tablet Support

So let's get started right at the beginning...

What You've Bought

While you already know that Amazon's Fire tablets are competitively priced compared to other tablets on the market, their real selling point is the way they integrate effortlessly with Amazon's enormous online store.

From its humble beginnings as an online bookstore, this ecommerce giant has grown into the world's largest retailer, and Amazon's digital content offerings have been a real success story too.

From your Fire tablet you can choose from well over 23 million media items, including books, movies, TV shows, apps and games, audiobooks, and music files. It's like holding the biggest library on the planet in the palm of your hand.

One of our favorite things about the Fire is that it's an Android-based tablet. Why is this so great? Because the Fire will run hundreds of free Android apps that you can download from the

Amazon App Store, along with hundreds more third-party apps.

It's true that the Android operating system has been altered by Amazon into a proprietary firmware for the Fire, so it won't run all of the Android apps in the Google Play app store. However, Amazon has built the device with a menu option to allow installation of non-Amazon apps, and we have been very satisfied with the results.

Please don't panic if, at this stage, all this tech jargon is a like a foreign language to you - by the end of this book you'll not think twice about using terms like "firmware" and "apps."

We wrote this Fire tablet book for complete beginners as well as Fire tablet veterans.

Our aim is not only to cover the how-to basics, but also to show you some of the lesser-known features of the Fire HD tablets that really make it fun to own.

All-New Fire HD 8 & HD 10 Specifications

Fire HD 8 and Fire HD 8 Plus

Screen size 8" (8" x 5.4 x 0.4")

Resolution 1280 x 800 189 ppi

Assorted colors: Black, Plum, Twilight Blue, White

Quad-core 2.0 GHz with 2 GB of RAM (Fire HD 8), or 3 GB (Fire HD 8 Plus

Dual stereo speakers optimized for Dolby Atmos

Built-in microphone

32 or 64 GB storage, expandable by up to 1 TB

Cameras: 2 MP front and rear facing camera

Dual-band single antenna Wi-Fi

Battery life up to 12 hours

Weighs 12.5 oz.

Customer support: screen sharing, email, web, and phone

Fire HD 10

Screen size 10.1" (10.3" x 6.3" x 0.4")

Resolution 1920 x 1200 224 ppi

Assorted colors: Black, Plum, Twilight Blue, White

Octa-core 2.0 GHz with 2 GB of RAM

Dolby Atmos, dual stereo speakers

Built-in microphone

32 or 64 GB storage, expandable by up to 512 GB

Cameras: 2 MP front and rear facing camera

Dual-band single antenna Wi-Fi

Battery life up to 12 hours

Weighs 17.8 oz.

Customer support: screen sharing, email, web, and phone

Fire Tablet Comparisons

So what's the difference between the Fire 7 and the new HD 8 & 10

Fire tablets and the other Fire models? Well basically the HD 8 & 10 are Amazon's premium tablet's and have the best specs.

As well as having the larger screen sizes they also boast Dolby Atmos sound and higher picture resolution and are therefore the best for users who intend to use their tablets for films, TV shows and music.

The battery life is improved, the processor a bit faster and the in-built cameras of a better quality than some earlier models. Given the quality of these tablets their prices are incredibly low. We love our Apple iPad but haven't upgraded to the latest version in ages due to the price. Conversely we didn't think twice about buying a new HD8 tablet for less than 90 bucks!

Do You Need To Buy the New 2020 HD 8?

If you've never bought a Fire tablet or are still using one of the much older models then the answer to this question, in our opinion, is definitely yes!

To buy a tablet of this size and quality for $89.99 just seems like a no brainer to us. And upgrading to the Fire HD 8 Plus for a further $20 to get that very useful extra RAM is also not that big a stretch. (Another advantage worth considering for the HD 8 Plus is that you can charge it wirelessly with the charging dock available for a further $20.)

If, however, you bought a Fire HD 8 more recently then the question requires a bit more consideration. The new HD 8 is an improvement on the earlier models but not so much that a casual user would notice much difference.

The main big difference (outside of the increased memory) is that the 2020 HD 8 now has the camera on the long edge of the tablet, prompting you to use it in horizontal mode for video calls and taking photos which takes a bit of getting used to (as on most other tablets the camera remains at the top for use in portrait mode). Horizontal mode makes good sense, though, for a lot of the major game apps and for watching video.

Furthermore, if you have an original Fire tablet, then you'll notice that the 2016 software update brought the voice-activated Alexa feature to the Fire tablet (more on that later in the book), and that feature remains in place with the 2020 model.

The two biggest advantages of the newer HD 8 are the price, $89.99 compared to the $150 you would have paid for the HD 8 in 2015, and the added memory. Internal memory now starts at 32 GB compared to 8 GB and for an extra $30 you can buy the 64 GB model.

For us as a family of four it was an easy decision to gift our 2017 HD8 to the kids for an upgraded replacement for just $90!

1. GETTING STARTED

Controls and Battery

Fire HD 8 and Fire HD 8 Plus

The 2020 Fire HD 8 and Fire HD 8 Plus have had a slight redesign, as follows:

The power switch is a black button located on the top mid-left of the Fire tablet when you hold it in the "portrait" position, with the long edges in each hand and the short edges at the top and bottom.

You will see the lens of the front-facing camera at the center of the left-hand long edge of the device. Thanks to the auto-rotate feature, your Fire HD tablet will display correctly in any position shortly after you power it up.

Fire HD 10

The power switch is a black button located on the top right of the Fire tablet when you hold it in the "portrait" position, with the long edges in each hand and the short edges at the top and bottom.

You will see the lens of the front-facing camera at the top center of the device. Thanks to the auto-rotate feature, your Fire HD tablet will display correctly in any position shortly after you power it up.

Power button   Microphone   Volume buttons

USB-C port   Headphone jack

Outside of these small differences, the two models work the same in terms of getting started!

- To turn on your device, press and hold the power button for 2-3 seconds.

- To put it to sleep while the power is on, touch the power button.

- To wake up the device, touch the power button and then slide your finger up from the bottom of the touchscreen.

- To turn it off, press and hold the power button and follow the prompt to either shut down or cancel.

- To adjust the speaker volume, press either of the two silver buttons on the top left edge: left to decrease and right to increase.

- To plug in a pair of Fire tablet headphones, earbuds or external speakers, use the pin jack on the top edge.

You will need battery power to operate your Fire, tablet so it's best to start charging it up as soon as you take it out of its box for the first time. A USB-C cable and 9W power adapter are included in the box. Plug the full-size end of the cable into the power adapter unit. Plug the USB-C end of the cable into your Fire HD's port located just to the left of the power button.

When your device is powered up, a lightning bolt will display inside the battery icon at the top right of the touchscreen to let you know the battery is charging. (You can also charge your Fire's battery from a USB 2.0 port of your desktop or laptop computer or a USB hub, but it will take longer than using the charger.)

The Fire HD's battery is claimed to last about 12 hours on full charge during average use and we have found this to be accurate, unless we're doing a lot of downloads or other power-hungry tasks. Charging a completely dead battery through the USB cable and power adapter takes about 5 hours.

The Fire tablet is designed for you to hold it in either portrait or landscape orientation, which gives you great flexibility in adapting the device to the tasks you're using it for. Even better, it changes orientation automatically along with you when you rotate it 90 degrees. You can even use it upside down!

The Fire HD tablet uses a touchscreen, so you will be navigating through the menus with your fingertips. There are two touch commands you will be using often, so take a moment to practice them on the Fire touchscreen.

Tapping means quickly touching your fingertip to an image on the screen, similar to clicking a mouse, and lifting it. You will tap once to select an item, such as a button, app icon, or block of text, and you will double tap to open an item.

Swiping means sweeping your finger across the screen. You will swipe to scroll, to turn a page, or to open menus.

When you turn on your Fire HD for the first time, it will automatically take you to an introductory demo screen that starts the registration process for the device. This screen will keep appearing until you register.

Setup and Registration

Your Fire tablet relies heavily on Amazon's cloud server, so your new device won't do much until you register it and link it with your Amazon user account. Registering allows you to wirelessly download your books, movies, games, apps, music, audiobooks, and other data that make your Fire tablet so much fun. Most new Fire owners will already have an Amazon account that they used to purchase their device, but if you received your Fire HD as a gift and don't have an account, you can set one up during the registration steps.

First, turn on your Fire HD, choose your language and tap *Continue*.

Next you will see a list of networks for connecting to the Internet. Your Fire tablet automatically scans for available wireless networks within range and lists them. Tap the network you want to use. Networks that require a password will have a lock symbol next to them, and you will need to know the password for that network (this is not the same as your Amazon account password).

If a wireless network password is required, the Fire's built-in onscreen keyboard will pop up so you can fill in the password box. The Shift key ⬆ on the keyboard is labeled with an upward arrow and lets you type capital letters. The ?123 key switches the keyboard layout between letters or numbers and symbols. When you tap this key, it will change the keyboard to numbers and symbols; tap it again to bring back the regular keyboard with letters.

When you have chosen a network, tap *Connect*. This network is now stored in your Fire, which will automatically find it and reconnect whenever it detects the signal.

Now that you are connected to the Internet, you will see a screen message that your Fire HD's system software is being downloaded and installed.

A Register Your Fire screen will appear. If you already have an Amazon account, type in the email address and password that you normally use to log in to that account. If you don't have an Amazon account, tap *Start here* under New to Amazon? to set up a new login and password with Amazon using the built-in keyboard.

Tap *Continue* and make sure the time zone displayed on your Fire tablet is the correct one.

If you see a Deregister button where the Register button should appear, you probably received your Fire HD tablet as a gift. Simply tap *Deregister* and go through the registration process above, using your own Amazon account information.

If you own other Fire devices, then setting up your new Fire tablet will give you the option to set it up with or without your content from a previous backup on another device. To transfer all of the content and settings from your other device to your new Fire tablet, tap *Choose Backup File*, tap the name of your previously registered device, and tap *Continue*. To set up your new Fire without adding your existing content, tap *Do Not Restore*.

If you've previously stored household profiles in your Family Library (see **Chapter 2**), an Import Profiles screen will appear. Tap the checkbox next to each profile to import it, or if you don't want to import it, uncheck the box by tapping it.

The Enable Location Services screen allows Amazon, some websites, and apps such as social media and maps to estimate your location. Tap *No Thanks* or *Enable* to set this service to your preference.

Next you will be prompted to link your Facebook, Twitter and Goodreads accounts with your Fire. You can do this now by clicking on the one or more of these social media links, entering your login and password for the social network, and tapping *Connect*. You can also skip this step for now by tapping *Continue*.

The Protect Your Fire screen appears next. This is an extended warranty protection plan for your Fire HD tablet device. If you're thinking of purchasing one of these plans, you don't need to do it during registration, but if you do buy it, it will take effect on the date your device was shipped to you no matter when you buy it. You can tap the *No Thanks* button to decline the plan, or tap the orange *Purchase* button to accept.

After registration, your Fire will run you through a very short tutorial about your device. Tap *Start* follow the orange prompts to move quickly through the tutorial, and tap *Exit* to end it, or simply tap *Exit* to skip the tutorial.

You will now see your "Home" screen. If you performed the Restore Your Fire step during the setup and registration process, then your Home screen will display any books and other media you have already purchased from Amazon. If you're tired of reading instructions and are anxious to get started actually using your Fire, tap one the content categories lined up across the top of your touch screen, such as books, apps or video, and tap a content icon to go ahead and open it!

Navigation

Here is a detailed anatomy of the Home screen and how to find your way around it.

The starting point for all of your navigation on your Fire tablet is the Home screen. If you ever get lost while navigating your Fire, tap the small hollow circle icon at the bottom of your screen once or twice to go back to Home.

If you can't see the circle, swipe toward the center of your screen from either the top or bottom edge.

Status Bar: Across the very top of the screen you will see icons and info about the status of your tablet. These include the Bluetooth icon, the Wi-Fi icon showing strength of your wireless network connection, the battery charge status, and the local time.

You will see other icons in this bar indicating your Fire tablet's settings when further features are activated (for example Airplane Mode). We will explain them in **Chapter 2**.

Search Box: This box, with a magnifying glass icon on the left, is always visible at the top of your screen below the Status Bar. It allows you to search the web, the Amazon store, or your Fire content library where the Amazon media items you buy are stored.

Tap this box and wait for the onscreen keyboard to appear. The onscreen keyboard pops up automatically for any task that requires text or voice command input. (We'll show you how to use the onscreen keyboard and voice command features in more detail in **Chapter 2**.)

To search by typing, type whatever you're looking for into the Search box. A list of choices will appear.

Tap a word or phrase from this list of suggested search terms that appears in the drop-down menu below the Search box.

To search by voice tap and hold the circle icon at the bottom of the screen until the blue line appears, then speak your word or phrase.

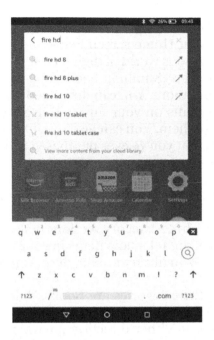

Your Fire HD will first look on the Internet for your Search box command and display the results on your screen. You can easily change your search to Amazon by tapping the center of the page above the Search results, or by swiping right to left. To search all of your stored Fire materials with the same command, tap *My Stuff* on the right side of the bar above the Search box, or swipe right to left again.

Category Bar: This display appears in white lettering across the top of your Fire tablet Home screen below the Search box. It's the gateway to the enormous world of digital content that awaits you as an Amazon user - over 38 million books, apps, games, movies, TV episodes, songs, and more. You can download and store thousands of Amazon media items on your Fire and use the Category Bar to access and organize them. You can also use it to access every single digital media item that you've ever purchased from Amazon, and of course to shop for even more content!

At the left end of the Category Bar are commands to display **For You** (recently accessed content) and **Home**, followed by several content categories. These category sections make it easier for you to find specific types of digital media items in your Fire HD downloads library, in your Amazon library online, or in Amazon's store.

From left to right, the categories are Books, Video, Games & Apps, Shop, Music, Audible, and Newsstand (for magazines and newspapers). Swipe in either direction anywhere on the screen to display the next category. Tap any category in the Category Bar to open it, display its contents and select an item.

When you open a content category (except for Shop), you will see a magazine-style browsing menu with rows of content customized for you based on your previous purchases and search history in Amazon. If you already own Amazon content in the category you've selected, some of those selections will display across the top row. Below you'll see an option to access your Library (see below) or the Amazon Store. Above the right side of most of these rows there's a **"See more"** link in small blue text that you can tap to display even more content.

The Shop category leads back to the search box, and will show products on sale at Amazon.

Library: Each content category has a Library icon both on the far-right side of the Category Bar and below. Tap it to view the content you already own in that category. The All option displays all of your content that Amazon safely holds for you in your online library (called Amazon Cloud). The "Downloaded" option only displays your content that you've downloaded and stored on your Fire device.

There is a further Search option at the top of the library page within any content category. If you wish to sort the order of your library content, use the sort icon which appears in Library view at the top right of your screen and looks like three graduated lines. Depending on the Category, the sort feature lets you switch your Library items in different ways, such as offering grid view or list view, or by recency or alphabetic order.

Store: The second icon on the right side of the Category Bar in each content category is a shopping cart and you can probably guess what that's for! Tap it to go to the Amazon Store section for that category, where you'll find recommended selections and several sub-categories that you can browse through. You'll also see recent releases, best sellers, and some special deals. You can use the Search box to find items in the Amazon Store with the onscreen keyboard or voice command. To shop in the entire Amazon store from your Fire, go back to the Home screen and tap *Store* in the Category Bar.

Sidebar Menu: There's a sidebar menu for each category that is only available in Library or Store view. To access the sidebar, tap any category in the Category Bar and tap the Library or Store icon. Tap the icon with three horizontal lines in the far upper left corner of the category next to its name . The sidebar menu features a wealth of sort options, sub categories, and settings. Your Fire's Email and Calendar apps also have sidebar menus with the some of the same navigation as the content categories. Swipe right to left to hide the sidebar.

New Items: Back on your Home screen, the section below the Category Bar displays randomly selected content that was recently delivered to your Fire tablet. These items can be quite random indeed, and their enormous icons really clutter up the touchscreen, so we prefer to remove them. To remove one or all New Items, press and hold that item. Tap *Remove from Home* to remove it from your home screen, or *Remove from Device* to delete it from your Fire. Deleting it from the screen display or your device won't remove it from your Amazon account, so you can always download it again.

App Grid: Apps are specialized software programs that perform specific jobs. The bottom half of your Home screen conveniently displays a grid of icons for every app installed on your Fire tablet. Swipe up or down to display all of the apps in your grid. Tap an app to open it.

To uninstall an app you downloaded and installed on your Fire, press and hold its icon until a checkmark appears, and tap *Uninstall* in the top right corner of your screen. (Apps that come preinstalled on the Fire HD tablet can't be uninstalled.)

The App Grid lets you change the order of your app icons or drop them into folders. Press and drag an icon to change its position. Drag one app icon on top of another to place it into a folder and give the folder a name using the onscreen keyboard or voice command. Tap the yellow checkbox on the keyboard to save the folder name.

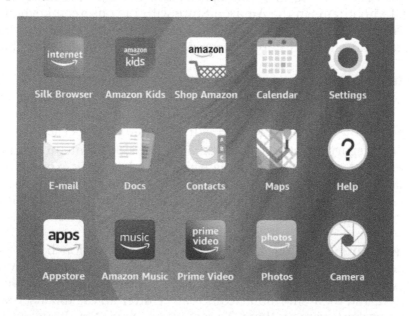

Navigation Bar: This is the black bar at the bottom of the Fire HD touchscreen that helps you navigate between menu screens.

To go back to the previous screen you were using, tap the hollow arrow pointing to the left ◁, just as if you were using a web browser.

To go back to the Home screen, tap the hollow circle icon ◎ once or twice. To display your recently opened apps in reverse order, tap the hollow square icon ▣. Tap **Home** to hide them.
To hide the onscreen keyboard, tap the hollow arrow pointing downward that appears whenever the keyboard is open.

If you don't see the Navigation Bar because your Fire tablet is in full screen view (for example, when you're reading a book), tap the center of the screen or swipe toward the center of your screen from the top or bottom edge.

Content Storage and Access

When you purchase and download digital content, such as an ebook, video, or app, from the Amazon Store, it is stored on your Fire as long there's enough space on its internal storage drive. Keep in mind that some of your Fire's storage space is taken up by its operating software, so not all of it will be available for storing your data.

The Fire HD comes with 32GB or 64GB of built-in data storage, but also has a microSD card slot, which expands the storage capacity up to 1Tb (for the Fire HD 8) or 512 GB (for the Fire HD 10).

You can use the microSD card to download and store videos, apps, games, and personal photos and videos. You can't use it to store web downloads from the Silk browser, or Email, so you'll have to use the Fire's built-in storage for those items.

The card slot is located on the long edge of the device when you hold it in the portrait position. Carefully pry off the slot cover and turn it slightly to show the slot.

With the top notch in the card facing upward, carefully slide the microSD card into the slot and push gently until it locks into place. Your Fire tablet will only work with certain types of cards. Amazon has provided a list of recommended cards that you can access from the Settings menu (see **Chapter 2).**

All About 'The Cloud': If you're new to the world of tablets, you might be confused by all the talk you've been hearing about "the cloud." To make things more confusing, Amazon has two cloud storage systems: the free storage you get as a customer for your Amazon content in Amazon Cloud, and Amazon Cloud Drive, which stores a certain amount of non-Amazon content for free and can be expanded for an annual sum. These are really two separate items, so let's try to clear up any confusion!

Amazon Cloud: Tablets like the Fire HD have much less internal data storage than a laptop or desktop computer, so they store most of their content online. Online data storage is called "the cloud" in tech lingo, and Amazon maintains its own cloud to store customers' digital content. Space in your Amazon Cloud library account is free and unlimited, as long as you only fill it with digital stuff you purchase from Amazon.

The great thing about Amazon Cloud is that you can free up internal storage on your Fire tablet at any time by deleting from your device any content you purchased from Amazon, knowing that Amazon will always keep a copy for you to download again at any time.

To download content from your Amazon Cloud library to your Fire, simply tap the appropriate content category in the Category Bar, tap *Library*, and tap the item's icon to download the file again.

Amazon Drive: This data storage service is a partly free/partly paid product that blends seamlessly with your free Amazon Cloud account on your Fire HD. Amazon Drive lets you store non-Amazon digital content that you already own, such as your personal photos, MP3 music files, home videos, etc. See **Chapter 8** for more info on how to use the Cloud Drive Desktop Application.

All Amazon customers get 5GB of storage free and Amazon Prime members get free unlimited storage on Amazon Drive for photos only, along with 5GB for videos and document files, and space for 250MB of non-Amazon music files.

The video and music storage fill up fast, but at least content purchases from Amazon don't count against this limit. There are also various plans for increased storage, starting at 100GB for $1.99 a month.

Cloud Collections: This Fire tablet feature lets you assemble your books, apps, games, audiobooks, and personal documents into one or more customized groups and store them in your Amazon Cloud library. Cloud Collections can be synced across all Amazon devices that support this feature. You can add as many items as you would like to each collection. Currently this feature doesn't support adding videos, music, newspapers, magazines, or photos.

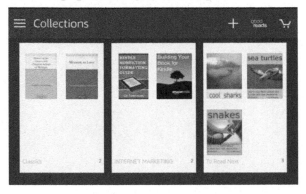

To create a new Cloud Collection, tap any eligible content category in the Category Bar, tap the *Library* or *Store* icon, then the tap on the sidebar menu, and tap *Collections*. Tap the + icon at the top right of the screen. Name the collection using the onscreen keyboard or voice command and tap *Create*. Tap one or more items you want to add to your collection and tap *Add* in the upper right corner.

To access a collection, display the sidebar menu in Library or Store view for any content category by swiping left to right, and tap *Collections.* Tap the icon for the collection you want to view.

To add a title to one or more Cloud Collections, tap the *Library* icon in any content category. Press and hold an item and tap the + icon in the upper right corner. Tap the checkbox next to each collection you want to add the item to and tap *OK*.

To rename a collection, press and hold the collection icon and tap the pencil icon in the top right corner. Type the new collection name into the field and tap **Rename.** To delete an item from a collection, open the collection, press and hold the icon, and tap the − *icon* in the top right corner. Deleting the item from the collection won't delete the item from your device.

To delete a collection, press and hold the collection icon and tap the trash can icon. This will delete the collection as a group but will not delete any of the items that made up the collection.

2. CUSTOMIZING YOUR SETTINGS

Your Fire has been programmed to automatically give you the best settings, but you can change them to your liking to match how you use your device. Although you won't be changing them often, they can make your navigation experience faster and less frustrating. The Fire tablet is small enough to go wherever you go, so we encourage you to make your Fire display uniquely you!

One very important function you should take care of right away is setting a PIN or password for your lock screen so no one can access your Amazon account and stored credit card information without your consent. Tap the **Settings** icon in the App Grid, scroll down to the Personal section, and tap **Security**. Tap **Lock Screen Passcode** and select whether you want to use a 4-digit numeric PIN, or a secure password. Confirm your PIN or password and tap **Finish**. Be sure to write down your PIN or password in a secure location for safekeeping.

Quick Settings Menu

This menu is hidden on your Home screen until you swipe down from the top edge of the screen to make it visible. From here you can easily adjust the settings you're most likely to use. To hide it again, swipe upward toward the top edge of the screen. Some of these menu items have sub-menus. To go back to the previous menu from within any sub- menu, tap the left arrow in the Navigation Bar at the bottom of the screen.

Brightness: Use the slider to adjust screen brightness.

Wireless: Detect and connect to or disconnect from a list of nearby wireless networks. Your Fire tablet will automatically connect to the network you most recently used if it's available.

Bluetooth: Tap the Bluetooth symbol and tap the switch icon to make your Fire HD tablet discoverable by a Bluetooth accessory or device. The Fire supports some wireless Bluetooth devices, including an external keyboard, mouse, speakers, or headset. It does not officially support Bluetooth microphones or headsets with a built-in microphone, but some of these may work on your device anyway.

Airplane Mode: Tap the airplane icon to quickly connect and disconnect from a wi-fi network. We turn off our wireless connection whenever we're not using it to save the Fire's battery life.

Blue Shade: This feature changes the color of your screen and blocks blue colors. The idea is that if you use this feature in the evening it puts less strain on the eyes and helps you fall asleep more easily after bedtime reading.

Do Not Disturb: Tap to quickly hide notifications and mute notification sounds.

Help: Lists the on-device Help options and Amazon Customer Service contact information. You can find more information about Amazon's support services in **Chapter 10**.

Alexa Hands-Free: Your Fire now come with Alexa and you can now operate Alexa hands free (more later). If you want to turn off hands free Alexa tap the icon here in the quick settings menu.

Settings: Tap the gear icon at the top of the quick settings drop down to access a long (very long!) list of additional settings for your Fire tablet. To make things less confusing for you, we cover this menu in a separate section below.

The Settings Menu

The Settings menu in the lower right corner of the Quick Settings menu offers you extra options that you may want to adjust to suit how you use your Fire HD, including things like customizing the Keyboard function and setting up Parental Controls. Here is a detailed explanation of each item on the Settings menu, as they appear from top to bottom on your Fire. The setting menu is a very long page so we have broken it up into three separate images.

Wireless: This is the same sub menu that appears when you tap *Wireless* directly from the Quick Settings menu.

Storage: This sub menu lets you quickly free up storage space by deleting items from your Fire HD tablet that you haven't recently used. These items will still be archived in your Amazon Cloud library. You can also use this menu to check how much internal storage you have left on your Fire, or to browse the Amazon Store for a recommended microSD card. If you have a microSD card, this is also the menu where you decide what content you want stored on your memory card.

Power: Conserve battery life by using this sub menu to manage functions that drain your Fire HD battery faster. We recommend enabling Automatic Smart Suspend, which turns off your wireless connection when you aren't using your device.

Apps & Games: This sub menu lets you manage your apps and see which ones are running. From here you can change an app's notification settings, delete old data that an app has stored on your Fire's hard drive to free up memory space, and change the way an app interacts with your other content libraries. You also may wish to disable Collect App Usage Data, which Amazon turns on by default to keep track of how often and how long you use your downloaded apps.

Display: This sub menu allows you to change your screen brightness and adjust the timeout period before the screen goes into lock mode if you don't touch it. You can also customize your Fire tablet touchscreen by adding a background photo. From the Display sub menu tap *Wallpaper* and select a photo from your photo library to display. Display Mirroring is another selection in the Display sub menu. It allows you to mirror your Fire display to compatible TV's and other media streaming devices, or an HDMI dongle such as the Fire TV Stick or Google Chromecast.

Alexa: This sub menu is where you can set Alexa. From here decide whether you want to use Alexa at all with your Fire (by toggling the option to access Alexa via the Home , whether you want to use the hands-free option (voice activated) and which wake word you want to use. If you don't want to use hands free then you will need to tap and hold the circle icon at the bottom of your screen to wake up Alexa before you can ask a question or give a command.

Device Options: This sub menu lets you check your Fire's serial number, see if its firmware version is up to date, back up your device, monitor the battery charge level, and change your time zone. You can also turn on the Find Your Tablet to enable Location Based Services so you can find your Fire remotely - not a bad idea in case your device is ever stolen.

The last adjustable option on the Device menu is **Reset to Factory Defaults**. This item wipes your Fire's hard drive completely clean in case you want to sell or give away the device - or if you forget your password and have to reset it (see **Chapter 10**). Treat this menu option with all due respect!

My Account: This sub menu controls how your Fire HD talks to your Amazon account. The e-mail address you see under this option is your Amazon account e-mail that you used earlier to register your Fire. If you want to deregister your device so you can sell it or give it away, tap the ***Deregister*** button. (To erase all content from your Fire's storage drive, use the Device Options sub menu.) You can also change some general email settings from this menu, manage Amazon account information and payment options, control your Prime membership, and manage how your Fire HD connects with Twitter, Facebook, and Goodreads if you skipped this step when you registered.

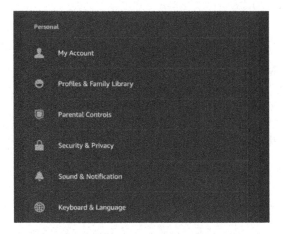

Profiles and Family Library: One Fire device can support unique profiles for up to 2 adults and 4 children. Users can select their own profile from the lock screen and have their own customized home screen, collections, preferences, apps, and content. This option lets each member of your family have a personalized experience on your Fire HD. Prime members can also share Prime benefits with other members of their household.

Parental Controls: If you want to restrict what other users can see on your Fire (and if, like us, you have kids who love the Fire as much as you do, then the answer is going to be yes!), tap ***Parental Controls*** in the Settings menu and again in the sub-menu. You will be prompted to enter a password. (It should be different from the one you use for the lock screen of your Fire tablet, and one that your kids are unlikely to guess!) *Confirm* and tap *Finish*. Important: be sure to write down your parental password and store it in a safe place. (See **Chapter 10** for what to do if you lose your password.)

Setting your parental controls password brings up a menu where you can give children and anyone else who doesn't have the password the ability to use only the Fire features you want them to use. You can use this menu to lock them out of the following functions on your Fire:

• Silk web browser

• Social networks

• Camera

• Amazon Maps app

• Email, Contacts, and Calendar apps

• Firefly app

• All Amazon purchases

• Amazon Video

• Specific content categories (for example, Books or Apps)

• Wireless network

• Location-based services

If you want to change any of these Parental Controls later on, or change your password, you will need to re-enter your password to unlock this menu. Parents should also check out **Chapter 4** for information about the Amazon Kids (formerly FreeTime) app and content delivery program for kids.

Security & Privacy: Here is where you set a password for your lock screen as we explain above. This is very important because your Fire is hooked up to your Amazon account and one-click purchasing. When your Fire powers up or goes into timeout, swipe the lock icon up from the bottom of your screen and enter your password to unlock it. Important: be sure to write down your password and store it in a safe place. (See **Chapter 10** for what to do if you lose your password.)

Another setting in the Security sub menu is Apps from Unknown Sources. If you want to install apps that aren't available in the Amazon store, you need to tap **On** for this option. (See **Chapter 4** for more information.)

Sound & Notification: This sub menu allows you to set which apps you want to receive notifications from - for example, whether you want your Calendar app to put a notification in your status bar to remind you of an appointment. The Do Not Disturb sub menu is identical to the one you can access directly from the Quick Settings menu to turn off notifications. You can also adjust your Fire tablet's speaker volume using the slider bar on this sub menu if you don't want to use the buttons on the outside of the case.

Keyboard & Language: You can change the language setting on your Fire HD by tapping **Language** from this sub menu and selecting your preferred language from the list. To customize the onscreen keyboard, tap **Current Keyboard Settings** and choose from several options. You can turn automatic capitalization and auto-correction on or off, and you can choose whether to enable Check Spelling to show suggested corrections and highlight possible misspellings.

You can also enable Next Word Prediction to predict words based on previously entered text, and download a different keyboard language. Finally, you can also turn on the Keyboard Sounds to get the effect of a mechanical keyboard. We both use this feature even though we feel a bit silly about it - it seems to help with the accuracy of our typing. Kids who grow up using only a touchscreen will wonder why this option even exists!

Sync Device: Tap to connect your Fire to your Amazon Cloud library and make sure all of the digital content you've ever purchased from Amazon is displayed in your Fire HD's content library menus. Sync also updates your Amazon books, movies, music, and other data that you've downloaded to your device's storage drive.

Help: This is the same sub menu that appears when you tap *Help* directly from the Quick Settings menu.

Accessibility: This sub menu allows you to adjust your Fire for enhanced vision and hearing capabilities. The Fire features Voice View natural language text-to-speech voice software to provide spoken feedback when you touch the screen and adjust the reading speed slower or faster. There's closed captioning for videos that have it, and a screen magnification command. The Voice View feature gives several accessibility shortcuts to help you navigate the touchscreen. These features are especially useful for people with disabilities.

Legal & Compliance: This sub menu has no user commands.

About Lockscreen Advertising

Part of the buzz when the first Kindle Fire was released concerned Amazon advertising. For a discount ($15 in late 2015), you can buy a Fire that displays advertising. (Or, put another way, for an extra fee you can buy a Fire with no ads.) We don't mind the ads. At least for now, they're unobtrusive, and if Amazon gets more aggressive about displaying them in the future, there's always the option of paying the fee to remove them later on.

Currently, the advertising appears on the Lockscreen when the device is locked. To unsubscribe from the Sponsored Lockscreen, you will need to go to the Amazon store from either the Fire Silk browser, or from the browser of your desktop computer.

Log in to your Amazon account, tap the small inverted triangle next to Your Account on the top navigation bar, and select **Manage Your Content and Devices** from the drop-down menu. Click the **Devices tab**, choose your device, scroll down to **Special Offers**, and click **Edit**. A window will pop up displaying the price to unsubscribe. From here it's just like making any other Amazon purchase. (Note that the Shop Amazon app on your Fire won't work for this process.)

If you want to see all of your offers at once, tap the **Amazon Offers app** on the App Grid. This app also lets you set your lockscreen offers to personalize based on your purchase and search history, and to filter lockscreen offers for inappropriate content.

Using the Fire HD Keyboard

One of the more interesting aspects of tablet technology is the fact that - mainly because of the limited space the screen affords - the onscreen keyboards are not fixed, but are dynamic, with the ability to change format depending on what you are typing. This means that the keyboard can do things like switch from letters to numbers and symbols (to do this on the Fire keyboard tap the numbers and symbols key ?123).

The keyboard interface is fairly self-explanatory for anyone who is familiar with the traditional Qwerty keyboard, but here are a couple of short cuts that may prove useful.

Delete: delete the character before the cursor by tapping the **delete key**, which is the back arrow with the "**x**" inside in the upper right corner of the onscreen keyboard. To delete all, hold down the *delete key*.

Hidden capitals lock: Double tap or tap and hold the ***shift key*** to keep letters in capital form. Tap ***shift*** again at the end when you want to unlock this function.

Quick access to numbers and symbols: When the keyboard is in letters format you will see small numbers at the top of the first row of letters. Tap and hold on the letter key for a second and you will see a button with the number. Lift your finger off the letter button and that number or symbol will automatically be inserted into your text.

Quick new sentence: Double tap the space bar at the end of a sentence to get a period followed by a single space and capitalization of the next word.

Punctuation shortcut: Tap and hold the period key to bring up a few other useful punctuation keys.

Dot com button: When you're using the Silk browser, or using email, and you type in a web or email address, a ".com" button appears on the keyboard next to the period button, and if you tap and hold on this button other domain name extensions appear (".org", ".net", etc).

Advanced symbols: When the keyboard is in numbers and symbols format, the shift button changes to a `~\<` key - tap on this to access less usual symbols such as foreign currency symbols, square brackets, percentage mark etc.

Editing shortcut: Tap and hold on an empty area near your text to access an Edit tool (which looks like a blue teardrop). Tap on this tool and drag it to the place in the text that you want to edit then lift your finger to release the tool and edit the section. When you're done, tap the edited section again to see the Edit tool - drag to the end of your text and release it to exit the function.

Cut, copy and paste: Tap and hold on a word to access and choose cut, copy or paste options - select more words by sliding the highlight teardrops. To paste your copied or cut text, tap and hold on the screen in the place you want to add the text and then choose the paste option.

3. USING THE INTERNET

If you have registered your Fire tablet, then you already have set up wireless access for it (see **Chapter 1**) through a Wi-Fi hotspot. You can manage your wireless networks from the Quick Settings Menu. Swipe downward from the top of your Fire screen and tap the Wireless icon to join a Wi-Fi network, switch networks, or disconnect wireless access to make your battery last longer.

Setting Up Email, Calendar, and Contacts

These three functions come as three separate apps on your Fire that are programmed to sync with each other. The Email app needs a bit of setup work before you can sync it with the other two applications. We're really pleased with the Fire HD's Email app that syncs with web-based email services like Gmail and Yahoo with just a few taps.

Setting Up Email: It's good to start by registering your Amazon account login email as your Fire's default email account, although you can start with any email account. Begin by tapping the Fire Email app from the Apps Grid on the Home screen. You will see the **Add Account** screen. Enter your email address using the onscreen keyboard and tap **Next**. Fill in your password and tap **Sign In**. Click **Accept** on the next screen to allow the Fire Email app access to your account, and wait for it to check your settings and register your email address. Your device will walk you through a short tutorial on how to use the Email app.

Now tap **Inbox** in the sidebar menu to see your email in that account. The app will populate your Fire Calendar and Contacts apps at the same time. Repeat the Add Account process if you want to add your other email accounts.

Fire's Email app easily links with Google Gmail, Yahoo, Hotmail, and other web-hosted email services and will also import your contacts and calendar from these accounts.

Linking to email providers that Fire doesn't recognize, such as your local broadband service, or your own domain name, is a bit more involved, but we were successful on the first try by opening our email client software on our computer, opening the Accounts menu, and duplicating the settings in our Fire Email app.

After entering your email address and password, the Fire Email app will ask you to choose whether to store this email as a POP3, IMAP, or Microsoft Exchange account. POP3 access downloads all of your emails to your device, while IMAP leaves them on your email provider's servers, allowing you to view all of your mail on any device you own. (Gmail also offers you the choice of accessing it as a POP3 or IMAP account, but you will need to configure this in Gmail through your web browser.)

Some users will need to set up an email account using Microsoft Exchange, especially if they need to check their workplace email account. Exchange might force you to set a password for your Fire lockscreen due to Microsoft's security requirements, but this is something you should do anyway (see **Chapter 2**). Once you've chosen which type of account you want to add, follow the Email app prompts to finish setting it up. Refer to your computer's email client software account settings as a guide, or use your Internet provider's support system.

Changing Your Email Settings: Once you've added your email accounts, you can change the settings from within the Email app by swiping from left to right to display the sidebar menu. You might need to scroll down on the sidebar to find the app's Settings menu. This menu lets you create separate settings for each of your email accounts and set some global options for all of your accounts, such as whether to display embedded images, automatically download attachments, and include the original message in your reply.

Within individual email accounts, you can choose whether to check your email manually, or automatically at a certain time interval.

You can customize each email account display name, which is what shows up in the "From" column when other people get email from you, and you can create an account-specific signature for your messages if you like. You should also name the email account you're setting up on the Fire so you can tell it apart from any other email accounts you set up on the device. The email applications menu also lets you specify how many messages you want the Fire to store on its internal storage drive.

The Settings menu in the sidebar also lets you add more accounts and change your default email account.

You can also remove an existing email account - just remember that removing an email account also removes all stored emails, contacts, and calendars.

Using the Email App: We were pleased to find that the Fire email app has all the familiar functions of other email programs we have used on our desktop and laptop computers. The app looks a bit different, but the commands are the same.

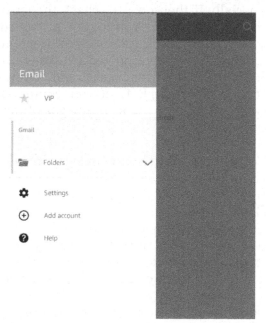

When you swipe from left to right, the Email app displays an Unread folder for your email accounts at the top of the sidebar menu, plus an Inbox folder and an Unread folder for each separate email account.

To show more folders, choose *Show Folders* for the account you want. (Gmail accounts will say Show Labels instead, since they don't use folders.) You can tap each folder's icon to look at its contents. Tap a single message to open it and read it.

The Email app checks your messages automatically at the interval you specified in the app's Settings menu. To check your email manually, go to the inbox screen and swipe downward.

To read a message, tap its subject line in your inbox. If you want to add the sender to your contacts, tap the sender's image in the email and tap *Add to Contacts*. You can also tap *Set as VIP* to add the sender to a separate list of VIP Contacts in the sidebar menu for quick reference.

If you want to read your messages from other devices, such as your smartphone or computer, then you might need to change some settings.

IMAP accounts, such as Gmail, Yahoo and Hotmail, automatically leave your messages on their servers until you delete them. POP3 accounts are a different story - your Fire tablet defaults to leaving messages on your POP3 server, but because POP3 servers don't automatically store your mail, it's a good idea to check the Incoming Settings sub menu for these email accounts to make sure!

To send a message, go to the lower-right corner of your Inbox screen and tap the pencil icon in the round blue circle ✐. Type an email address in the *To* line. If that person is already on your list of contacts, the app will suggest an address. To add a new address to your contacts, tap the **+** *icon* to bring up Contacts and save it. Now type in a subject line and type your message. Tap the *Send arrow* icon, or *Cancel* to delete.

To reply to or forward an open message, tap *Respond* and choose from *Reply*, *Reply All*, or *Forward*. Enter a To address and subject line, type your message, and tap Send.

To add an attachment to an outgoing email, tap the paper clip icon in the upper right corner and then tap *Attach a Photo*, *Attach a File*, or *Capture a Photo*. The Fire email app lets you attach documents, photos, and even music tracks you purchase from

Amazon and download to your device.

To download or open an attachment to an email you have received, view the message, tap the **download icon**, and tap and hold the attachment to open or save it. The attachment will save to your Documents library, which you can access from the Documents app in the App Grid.

To delete a message, tap the checkbox next to any message you want to delete; then tap the **Delete** trashcan icon. To save a draft of a message, tap the menu icon with three vertical dots in the upper right corner and tap **Save Draft**. Tap **Discard Draft** using the same icon to delete.

To add a custom signature, swipe left to right to open the sidebar menu, and then tap on your email account; you'll then see a Signature option where you can add your personal sign-off message/ signature.

Calendar: The Fire tablet's Calendar app looks and acts like any other standard calendar software, but it has one extra-cool feature: it can sync with many online calendars such as Google Calendar and Yahoo Calendar. This allows you to work from the same calendar no matter which device you are using. Some Windows Live accounts are not supported by the app.

To open the Calendar app, find and tap it in the Apps Grid.

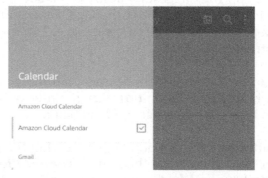

Contacts: This address book app syncs with your online email accounts. To open it, find and tap it in the Apps Grid. You can import and export your contacts to or from another app or change the way the app sorts names by tapping the menu icon with three vertical dots in the upper right corner. Tap **Import/Export**, or tap **Settings** to set your Contacts options.

Using the Fire Silk Browser

Amazon's Silk browser comes pre-installed on the Fire HD. Part of this browser's functioning takes place on Amazon's enormous Cloud Drive, which works in tandem with your Fire tablet to make your web surfing a smooth ride.

Open the browser from the Home screen by tapping the **Silk Browser** icon from the Apps Grid.

The browser window will open with a starter screen that displays Amazon as a default bookmark. To get started with browsing, either type a search term or web address into the Search box at the top of the screen, or use the voice command.

The layout is fairly intuitive for anyone who uses the Internet, with tabbed browsing, bookmarks, and browsing history. The only thing that initially confused us is that the Back arrow is at the bottom of the browser window, in the Navigation Bar, instead of at the top.

Basic Search: Silk combines the Search box with the web address box, similar to Google Chrome. To search the web, tap the *Search box* to bring up the onscreen keyboard.

Type your search term into the box or use the voice command and tap the big orange arrow key on the right hand side of the keyboard to get your search results. Tap a result to open that web page. You can also type a website address directly into the box, or type in a partial address and choose from the list of options that the browser brings up.

Tabbed Browsing: Tap the + *key* in the upper right corner of the browser window if you want to open a new tab to browse in. To open a link in a new tab on an existing search result or web page without leaving that page, tap and hold the link and choose *Open in New Tab* from the pop-up menu.

To close a tab, tap the *X* in the right corner of the tab. To display the Starter screen when the Silk browser is already open, close each open browser tab by tapping the *X*, or tap the + *key* to open a blank tab.

Bookmark a Page: Tap the ribbon icon, marked Bookmarks, in the bottom left hand tab to bookmark a page. To view your bookmarks, swipe from left to right to display the sidebar menu and tap *Bookmarks*. To visit a bookmarked page, tap its listing. To delete a bookmark, tap and hold its listing, tap *Remove bookmark* on the pop-up menu, and tap *Remove*.

View Your Browser History: Tap the middle bottom clock tab, marked *History*, to see a list of sites you have visited in the past seven days. If you want to delete your history, tap the *trash can icon* in the upper right corner of the History menu and check the types of history you want to delete.

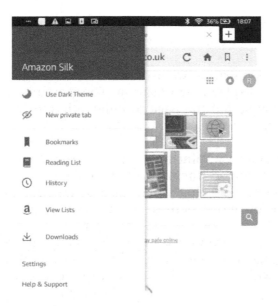

Personalize Your Browser: Tap the three horizontal lines at the top of the page, to the left of the search box, to bring up a number of customization options for the Silk browser.

You can choose between a light and a dark theme for your browser, opening a private bowser window, accessing bookmarks and reading lists and recent browsing history.

This is also where you will find the Silk browser settings where you can set the search engine you prefer to use, manage passwords and set your preferred privacy settings.

Most websites have versions designed for mobile browsing. Their looks and functionality are improving, but we still feel that the Fire screen is big enough to handle the desktop versions of sites like Facebook and CNN.

To choose a different viewing option, tap the menu icon with three vertical dots on the right side of the search box and toggle between *Request Desktop Site* or *Request Mobile Site*.

Note that the Silk browser doesn't support Flash streaming video, but sometimes you can solve this problem by switching to Mobile

View. Some popular websites may have their own apps that allow you to view their video content on the Silk browser.

One personalization feature we use often is enlarging or reducing the browser page display magnification. There are two ways to do this. You can double tap the page to enlarge it and double tap it again to reduce it.

The other method is "pinching": place two fingers on the touchscreen and spread them apart to enlarge, or pull them together to reduce. Note that you'll need to wait for the page to finish loading before either of these methods will work.

Another very cool feature we use on the Fire tablet is the ability to share any web page in an email directly from the Silk Browser. Tap the menu icon with three vertical dots in the search bar with the page open and tap the Share option on the menu.

It's a good way to share your discoveries on the web with friends and professional contacts who don't use Twitter or Facebook.

Using Other Search Engines: The Fire Silk browser defaults to the Bing search engine, but if you prefer to use Google, or Yahoo, you can change the default search engine setting. Swipe from left to right, tap **Settings**, **Advanced**, and tap **Search Engine** to choose your new default search engine.

Shopping on Your Fire Tablet

The Fire device makes shopping on Amazon incredibly easy, which is yet another smart marketing strategy for them. You can shop for digital content from within each content category on your device, or you can use the Amazon shopping app to shop the entire Amazon website at once. For digital content purchases from Amazon, you first must enable a 1-Click Payment Method in your Amazon account. (This is true even if you are downloading free content or apps.)

Setting Up 1-Click Payment: You will need a credit card on file with Amazon to complete this task. Open the **Settings** menu from the Apps Grid, tap **My Account**, tap **Amazon Account Settings**, and tap **Payment Options**. Log in to your Amazon account and tap the **Edit link** to change your 1-Click Payment options.

Shopping for Digital Content: Each of the content categories on the Fire Home screen has its own app for accessing the Amazon store. Pick a content category, tap **Store**, and a new screen will open to take you on a shopping spree in that content category. For example, if you go to the Home screen, tap **Apps**, and tap **Store**, the Amazon App Store will load on your screen.

The main page of each store app will feature freebies and special sale items, with suggestions for items you might want to buy based on your past search and purchase history with Amazon.

There is an option to look at Best Sellers, and an option for New Releases. Each store's main page also includes a Search box.

If you already know what you want to buy, tap the Search box to bring up the onscreen keyboard and type in the name of your item, or use the voice command.

Click the Buy button to purchase the item with your 1-Click Payment method and download it to your Fire tablet.

If you don't want to buy an item right away, you can tap the More Options button and tap **Add to Wish List** so you can come back to it later. To see your Wish List, swipe from left to right and tap **Wish List** to bring up your list.

Shopping on Amazon: There are two ways to shop on the entire Amazon site from your Fire. The first way is to go to the Home screen and tap Shop in the Category Bar. This option appears in the center of the Category Bar, and we don't think this is any accident!

The other way to shop is to tap the **Shop Amazon app** in the Apps Grid. Either way, the user experience is very similar to shopping on Amazon from your desktop or laptop computer.

Don't Forget Amazon Prime: Your Amazon account comes with a free month of Amazon Prime (unless you've already used up this option). This opens up all kinds of free content possibilities, including the Fire ebook lending library and Prime Instant Video, plus you get free 2-day shipping on your non-digital Amazon orders.

There are special categories of Prime membership, such as student and parent, which have some restrictions on free content, so be sure to do a bit of research before you pay the fee and buy into the program.

4. USING APPS

Applications, which we call "apps" throughout this book, are mini software programs that perform specialized tasks on your smartphone or tablet. Because they are so specific, they run lean and don't take up much room on your Fire HD's internal storage drive. There are apps for just about every task you can think of, and probably some you haven't thought of yet! Apps really are what make your Fire fun.

The operating system on your Fire HD is based on the Android operating system, which puts thousands of Android apps at your fingertips.

Not all of them - unfortunately some Android apps just won't run on the Fire - but you still have thousands to choose from, and you can download them right from the Amazon App Store to your Fire HD tablet. The best part is that a lot of them are free!

For the inside track on some of the best apps available, check out our companion book, - **250+ Best Kindle Fire and Fire HD Apps for the New Kindle Fire Owner. (www.amazon.com/dp/B08PBVX3LW)**

The Fire HD tablet ships with several apps pre-installed, with their icons displayed in the App Grid. They include:

- Silk web browser app

- Amazon Kids (formerly FreeTime) app

- Email, Contacts, and Calendar apps

- Weather app

- Maps app

- Calculator app

- Clock app

- Shop Amazon app

- Amazon Offers app

- Specific Amazon store apps for Kindle, music, Audible audiobooks, video, games and apps

- Goodreads app

- Fire HD device apps for camera, documents, videos, and photos

- Washington Post app

Help app and Settings app: These are simply shortcuts to the same items found in the Quick Settings Menu. (See **Chapter 2**)

Amazon Kids (formerly FreeTime): This app comes pre-installed on your Fire and lets you set up a custom selection of content for up to 4 kids. Simply follow the prompts to create separate profiles based on that child's individual preferences and assign your choice of books, apps, and videos to each profile.

The Amazon Kids app itself is free, while Amazon Kids+ is a monthly subscription service for the app that delivers Amazon-selected children's videos, books, educational apps, movies, and television shows.

This is very smart marketing on Amazon's part - they are introducing very young users to the Fire HD in hopes of making them users for life.

Amazon Kids content is aimed at children ages 3 through 8 and is drawn from big-name kids' media producers like Disney, Sesame Street, Nickelodeon, and even PBS, so your kids can combine learning with entertainment.

There's also a teen profile option aimed at young people ages 11 through 17. The per-user price is quite reasonable, and with Amazon Prime, it's even better.

Get Your Game On

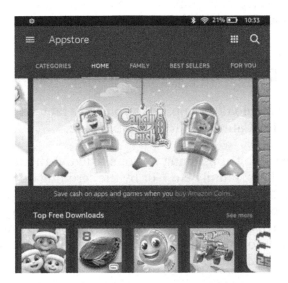

Amazon classifies its downloadable games as apps, so they appear in two content categories: in the app category with all kinds of other apps, and in the games category, which displays only games. To access this library, tap **Games** in the Category Bar.

Tap **Store** to see which games Amazon is promoting on the Games page, and use the search box and on-screen keyboard or voice command to find the games of your choice. More categories of games are available when you swipe left to right to bring up the sidebar menu.

Many games have a Test Drive button that allows you check the game out for a short time before you download it.

Tap the price button to purchase the game, and then tap **Download** to download it to your device where it will appear in both the All and Downloaded libraries.

Like all other Fire apps, games must actually be stored on your device before you can use them.

Worth noting here, the latest **Game Mode** feature is available on the new 2020 Fire HD 8 tablet; enabling Game Mode allows you to play games without any pesky interruptions such as email notifications distracting you! To enable this feature go to **Settings**, select **Apps & Games** and then **Game Mode** to **On**.

Downloading Apps from Amazon

To find and download an app, go to your Fire tablet's Home screen, tap **Apps** in the Category Bar, and tap **Store**.

You can search for apps using options listed at the top of the App Store (Bestsellers, Family etc.) or by the scrolling down in the App Store, where you'll see New Releases and apps that are Recommended for You based on your browsing history. Swipe from left to right to display the sidebar menu, where you'll find even more ways to search for apps. Tap the app's icon to read its description and learn more about it.

If you're anxious to get started and don't want to read more right away, you might want to start by downloading some popular free apps from the App Store.

Tap the magnifying glass icon at the top of the App store window to open the search box and onscreen keyboard or voice command. You can find apps like Netflix, the Weather Channel, ESPN ScoreCenter, and more, along with a number of games.

Free apps are downloaded with Amazon's standard 1-Click Ordering, but your account will show a charge of $0.00. (Remember that Netflix has "in-app purchase" meaning that it charges its own monthly subscription fee for you to use the app to stream video.)

You might notice some small print in the App Store telling you that you have some Amazon Coins to spend on apps and games. This is virtual money that Amazon manages for you so you can use it to buy... you guessed it...more apps! Amazon makes a token Coins deposit for you when you register your Fire tablet, and you can purchase more Coins by swiping left to right and choosing Amazon Coins from the sidebar menu.

When you find an app you want to download, it is a good idea to check out the developer's reputation by seeing if they provide their company name, and whether they are selling other apps besides this one.

With an app that is advertised as free, make sure that it really is completely free or whether an additional fee is required (called an "in- app purchase") to use it. Make sure you understand the permissions you have to give this app to work on your Fire.

It seems like overkill, and we don't always do it ourselves when downloading well-known apps, but those "freebies of the day" often come out of nowhere. So trust, but verify!

To download an app, tap the price button near the description. If the app isn't free, your 1-Click Ordering account will be charged and the button will change to *Get App*. Free apps actually register as a sale in your 1-Click Ordering account, but the amount shows as $0.00. Tap the Get App button and the app will be automatically downloaded to your Fire tablet.

When it finishes, tap the *Open* button to use it. If you don't want to use it right away, you can find it later by tapping *Apps* from the Home screen Category Bar to look for it.

If you have downloaded or opened it recently, it also will appear in the Apps Grid. Note that apps must be downloaded to your Fire tablet before you can open them, unlike the other content categories on the Category Bar.

You can also buy Fire apps from your PC or Mac computer's browser and have them sent directly to your Fire. Your Amazon account will automatically detect that you have a Fire registered and will send your download directly to your device. As soon as you power up your Fire, or tap Sync Device from the Settings Menu, the app will download and open.

The Amazon App Store lists about 30 categories of apps. All these selections can be overwhelming, so we suggest that you go with a basic list at first and round out your selections later on.

One good rule of thumb for downloading apps is to look at the Amazon customer reviews. Apps that average 3 stars or fewer, or have very few reviews, are probably (but not always) not as good a bet as an app with hundreds of good reviews.

Here is our favorite "must-have" list for your first visit to the Amazon App Store. Again, if you're outside the US don't use the links but search for them by name via your Fire tablet search box or at the app store at **Amazon.co.uk**

Netflix (https://www.amazon.com/dp/B00OGRMULA) - lets you watch movies and TV shows on your Fire when you order the in-app subscription or use your existing subscription information. If you're new to this service, downloading the free app gives you a one-month free trial. Note that Hulu, Sling, Disney+, Philo, HBO GO and NOW, Starz, DC Universe and Showtime apps are also available to use in combination with your subscription on the Fire tablet.

Skype (https://www.amazon.com/dp/B008M721MS) or **Zoom (https://www.amazon.com/dp/B00B5L5JRM)** – Whilst Amazon do have their own video calling service via the Alexa app, you can only make calls to other people who also have Alexa! So if you need a wider reaching video call service, for meetings and so on, or you've already have a Skype or Zoom account, then you can download the relevant app from the Amazon App Store to use those services on your Fire tablet.

Spotify (www.amazon.com/dp/B00KLBR6IC) - You will never run out of new music to discover when you connect to Spotify. With their free or premium service you can listen to favorite artists or albums or simply choose a playlist that suits your mood.

TuneIn (www.amazon.com/dp/B004GYY714) - If you like listening to the radio for talk or music then prepare yourself for Tunein. With over 100,000 real radio stations and more than four million podcasts streaming it's safe to say there's something for everyone.

Skype (www.amazon.com/dp/B008M721MS) - Stay in touch with friends in family via Skype. WhatsApp isn't available for your Fire tablet so Skype is your best option for now.

AccuWeather (www.amazon.com/dp/B005K17RU0) - is the stand-out app for keeping abreast of the weather where you are. Updated every 15 minutes with an attractive interactive layout, download for free and make sure you never get caught in the rain again.

Angry Birds (www.amzn.to/3mdxxF7) - is the most popular game app franchise in the world. Help the colorful birds heap payback on the green pigs. Be sure to download a Fire Tablet edition. The basic version is free, but there are numerous upgrades that aren't.

Paint Pad HD (https://www.amazon.com/dp/B00EXFHQ7S) - get creative anywhere, no matter what your level or age, if you love to draw or doodle you'll love this arty app.

Minecraft (www.amazon.com/dp/B00992CF6W) - If you don't know what Minecraft is...ask your children/grandchildren!

Flow Free (www.amazon.com/dp/B008JGSM6G) - A gentle but satisfying game, just connect the matching colors to create your free flowing pipe network. Starts off easy but soon gets tricky.

For a whole lot more great apps, both free and paid, to suit just about every conceivable need, you can also check out our companion book **-250+ Best Kindle Fire and Fire HD Apps for the New Kindle Fire Owner. (www.amazon.com/dp/B08PBVX3LW)**

Uninstalling Apps

If you download a lot of apps, your Fire tablet's data storage will fill up quickly. It's a good idea to do a bit of housecleaning once a month or so and get rid of any apps you aren't using.

Remember that any app you order from Amazon will always be available in your Amazon Cloud library if you want to download and re-install it.

Alternatively remember that you can now buy a microSD memory card and slip it into the microSD slot on the side of your Fire HD tablet to store your games and apps there.

To uninstall an app, tap the **Apps** content category in the Category Bar. Tap **Library** and tap **Downloaded**. Tap the menu icon with three vertical dots next to the app you want to remove and tap Delete from Device.

The app is now gone from your Fire tablet but still stored safely in your Amazon Cloud library.

Once you have uninstalled an app, it won't be updated when you sync your device unless you manually re-install it.

To re-install, tap **Apps** in the Navigation Bar, tap **All**, and tap the orange arrow icon to download it.

Apps stored on your Fire tablet are visible in the Downloaded section of the Apps Library.

Be careful **NOT to tap** Delete from Cloud and delete a paid app from your Cloud library, or you will have to buy it again to re-install it!

Force-Closing Apps

If an app stops working, the best solution is to just force-close it. Sweep down from the top of your screen to open the Quick Settings Menu. Tap **Settings**, tap **Apps & Games** and then tap **Manage All Applications** to bring up a list of the apps installed on your Fire. Tap the icon for the stuck application and tap Force Stop to close it.

Installing Third-Party Apps

At first it may seem as if the selection of apps in the Amazon store is endless, but in reality, Amazon offers only a small percentage of the more than 500,000 apps available for Android. For a taste of what you're missing, take a look at the selection in the Google Play App Store (play.google.com/store/apps) and see if it seems worth your while to install apps on your Fire from outside the Amazon App Store.

This process isn't always straightforward, and some Android apps simply won't work on your Fire, but it's worthwhile if you have a bit of tech skill or you don't mind spending some time to figure it out.

Note that we're not talking about "rooting," which involves installing new firmware on your Fire to enable the installation of third-party apps. Rooting will void your Fire warranty and open you up to all kinds of operating problems unless you really know what you're doing.

Amazon has built a menu item for installing third-party apps on your Fire, so it's safe to say they allow it. Tap *Settings* in the Apps Grid, then tap **Security**. Tap **Apps from Unknown Sources** and so the switch icon turns orange. This sets up your Fire tablet to install apps from sources outside of the Amazon App Store.

Be sure to download and install an Android Security App as described earlier in this chapter before you go any further. This is especially critical with online app stores, where an app can come from just about anywhere.

Some good places to find apps include the Bemobi Mobile Store - (**ovi.sigma.apps.bemobi.com**) - operated by the company that developed the Opera browser and SlideMe - (**www.slideme.org**). Both of these sites feature Android apps for downloading and are high profile enough to reduce the risk of installing something buggy.

If you want to transfer apps from another device to your Fire, first go to the Amazon App Store and install the ES File Explorer app (**www.amzn.to/3gH0Bni**) on your Fire HD tablet.

This nifty app lets you manage the stored files on your Fire just as you would on your Mac or PC. Next, use the file explorer software on your desktop or laptop computer to transfer the app files you want from your Android phone or other device to your computer's hard drive.

Look for the extension .APK, which is the Android app file extension. Then transfer the app from your computer to your Fire, either with the mini USB cable, or as an attachment in an email to yourself (See **Chapter 8** for details of how to do this). Finally, use the ES File Explorer app to find and install each new app.

Non-Amazon apps don't install and open automatically like the ones you download from the Amazon App Store. There are three different methods we use to find and open Android apps on our Fire tablet.

Web Downloads: Open the Silk browser from the Apps Grid. Swipe from left to right to display the sidebar menu. Tap the Downloads button and look for your Android app, which should show an .APK extension. Tap it to install. If you get an error message, try tapping Notifications.

View Notifications: Look in the status bar across the top of your screen for a small number in a circle just to the right of your device name. If you see one, swipe the status bar down to see your notifications. If your Android app appears in the list with the .APK extension, tap it and see if the app will install.

File Exploring App: If neither of the above options work, install the ES File Explorer app as we describe above and open it. You should see several rows of blue folders. Locate the one marked Downloads and tap it to see the contents. Locate the app with the .APK extension and tap it to install.

If the installation process starts, you will need to read and accept permissions for that app and wait for the installation to complete. After that, tap *Open* at the bottom of the installation screen. If all goes well, your Android app will behave just like the Amazon apps on your Fire from now on.

We have found that the Fire gets mixed results with apps that we downloaded to our Android phone from Google Play - some of them only work partially on our Fire tablet, and some don't work at all. But it's the closest thing to putting Android functionality on your Fire that you can get without rooting, and we kind of like the challenge!

5. READING BOOKS AND NEWSSTAND ITEMS

Amazon got its start in the book selling business, and nobody does it better. It has the largest database of book titles in the world, and the bookstore is a great place to browse and do research. Amazon's development of the Fire tablet as an ebook reader was another history-making event. The technology has grown so quickly that looking at our Fire tablet today it's hard to believe that the original device was a simple e-reader with a black and white screen that could only display ebooks!

Buying Books from Amazon

The first thing you will see when you are viewing the **Books** category page on your tablet is a selection of books from your Books Library (if you have any). Below that you will see links to your full **Library** and the **Store**. To shop for ebooks on Amazon, tap **Store**.

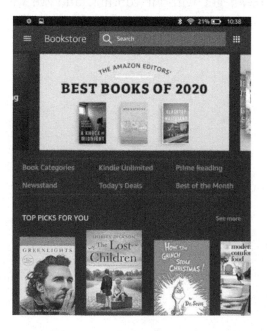

The **Books Store** will show a scrolling menu of current Best Sellers and book related offers, and then under that a selection of search categories followed by various other suggestions such as Recommended for You lists (which Amazon carefully puts together from your previous search and buying history) and lists of Best Sellers. You can browse the Book Store using any of these categories.

You may also see books from the Kindle Unlimited program. This is a paid subscription program that gives you access to about 800,000 ebooks for a $9.99 monthly subscription fee. If you're interested, there's a 30-day free trial.

To learn more about a book, tap its cover. From the book's information page, you can read its description and see its Amazon reader reviews. Tapping the Download Sample button will download a sample excerpt to your Fire. Tap the Read Now button when the download finishes to see if it is something you want to buy.

To mark a book to look at later, tap the More Options button and tap Add to Wish List, which will store it in your Amazon Wish List. To see your Wish List, swipe from left to right to display the sidebar menu and tap Wish List to display the list.

To search for a certain book title, tap the magnifying glass icon at the top of any Book Store page to display the Search box and type the book's title, author, or keywords into it using the Fire's onscreen keyboard or the voice command. You can also search the book database by its ISBN number.

To buy and download a book, tap the Buy button near the description. Amazon will charge your 1-Click Ordering account for the price of the book and the button will change to say Downloading. If you are downloading a free title, it will still register as a sale in your 1-Click Ordering account in the amount of $0.00. When the download is complete, the button will change again to say Read Now. Amazon gives you the option of canceling your order if you bought the book by mistake.

You can also buy Kindle ebooks from your PC or Mac computer and send them directly to your Fire. Your Amazon account will automatically know that you have a Fire registered and will list your device in the drop-down menu marked "Deliver to" on the right side of your browser screen under the Buy button. Select your Fire from the list, and as soon as you power up your Fire, or tap **Sync Device** from the Settings Menu, the book will download and open.

Reading Books on Your Fire HD

Any new, unopened books on your Fire tablet will appear in your Books Library with a strip across the cover that says New. You can find your newly purchased books by tapping **Books** from the Home screen Category Bar.

If you are in the process of reading a book, the cover will display the percentage of the book you have finished so far. Double tap the cover icon that appears in your Library to open the book and read it, or tap it once and wait for it to open automatically.

Turn the pages by swiping in the direction you want to move, or tapping the side of the screen.

When you open a book to read, the Fire defaults to full screen mode and hides all navigation icons, which can leave you feeling stranded until you learn how to escape. Simply tap once anywhere on the book page, or swipe from the top or bottom of the screen. The Navigation Bar with the Home and Back icons will appear at the bottom, and the Reading Toolbar will appear at the top. You will also see a slider showing how much of the book you've finished.

You can use the slider as a Go To command to move to a numbered location within the book. If you swipe left to right while these menus are visible, you'll bring up a full table of contents that you can tap to go to the beginning of each chapter. Tap the page again to hide these menus.

Word Runner: Some readers find this feature really speeds up their reading by displaying words one at a time in large print at a pace present to their individual reading style.

To enable it, tap the menu icon with three vertical dots on the Reading Toolbar, tap *Word Runner*, and tap the forward arrow to play. Drag the speed bar to adjust the display speed. If you tap and hold the screen, it will activate the Brake so you can catch up. Note that not all books are able to access this feature.

Managing Your Book Library: Books can really fill up your Fire's data storage, so Amazon gives you two tabs at the top of your

Book Library screen. Titles displayed in the All tab are your complete collection of book purchases stored in your Amazon Cloud library, while the titles shown in the Downloaded tab are the ones you have downloaded from your Amazon Cloud library to your Fire device.

If you want to read a book from the cloud that you haven't stored on your device, then you can only access it when your Fire is connected to a wireless network. This leaves more data storage space open on your Fire, but remember that you can't access the cloud while reading at the beach.

If you plan to travel to a location with no wireless access and want to read on your Fire, do a bit of advance planning and download the books you want to read so they are stored on your device.

To download or remove a book from your Fire, tap **Books** in the Category Bar and tap **Library**. To download a book from your Amazon Cloud library, tap **All**, and tap the book's cover to download it.

To remove a book from your device, tap Downloaded, and press and hold on the cover until a trash can icon appears in the upper right corner of your screen. Tapping the trash can icon takes the book off your Fire tablet but leaves it in your Amazon Cloud library to download again at any time. Don't delete any books from your library in the cloud, or you will have to buy them again to download them.

Fire HD Reading Accessibility Features

The Fire tablet ebook reader app lets you customize your reading experience from the Reading Toolbar. To display the toolbar, tap the screen while displaying any book in the reader. From here adjust the appearance of the reader screen via the options across the top. Tap **Aa** to customize the reader's background and text colors, enlarge or reduce the text size, change the display font, and even change the spacing.
If you tap the menu icon with the three vertical dots and choose

Additional Settings, there are also some other very interesting options and functions here to choose from which can greatly improve your user experience. These include:

Text-to-Speech: For those books that are Text-to-Speech enabled, this button will let your Fire read text to you! To access it, tap the menu icon with three vertical dots on the Reading Toolbar, tap *Additional Settings* at the bottom, and tap *Text-to-Speech* to turn it on for books that are enabled for this feature.

X-Ray: This is a great tool for reading club fans and students. In books that are X-Ray enabled (not all books are), you can use this option to find passages in a book that mention the same concept, character, places and other useful information about the book or the author. To access it, tap any page that you are on and if the book is X-Ray enabled you will see a small page icon with a black 'x' in it amongst the icons at the top of the page.

Share: The Share option on the Reading Toolbar is a super quick way for you to copy and share sections of a book via Twitter or Facebook.

Bookmark: Simply tap the upper right corner of the book page to create a bookmark on the page you're currently reading. Fire will automatically go to this page when you next open that book. To display your bookmarks, tap anywhere on the book page to bring up the Reading Toolbar and tap the *Bookmarks icon* on the right.

Making notes and highlighting text: Tap the screen on the first word of a section you want to highlight, then drag your finger along the section. Lift your finger and an option box will pop up asking you what you want to do with the section (either add a note, highlight or share). You can access your notes and highlights via the Notes option on the Reading Toolbar. You can also see sections of a book that other readers have highlighted by turning on the Popular Highlights option. Swipe downward from the top edge to display the Quick Settings Menu, tap *Settings*, and tap *Apps & Games*. Tap the *Amazon Application Settings* sub menu, tap *Reader Settings*, and tap *Popular Highlights* to turn it on or off.

Dictionary: The reader app also features a built-in dictionary. Tap and hold any word to bring up a quick definition. If you click *Full*

Definition, the dictionary will expand to show you the complete entry within the dictionary. The dictionary lets you search the book for the word, search on Wikipedia, or search the web for it. You can also translate the word by typing your own language into the translate box in the corner of the definition box and selecting the language you want to translate it into - neat!

Word Wise: When activated, this feature shows brief inline hints for unknown words in a book. You can set the word difficulty level

Feudal and monarchical maladies no longer run in our

blood. There is no more of the Middle Ages in our

constitution. We no longer live in the days when terrible

swarms within made irruptions, when one heard beneath

his feet the obscure course of a dull rumble, when

indescribable elevations from mole-like tunnels appeared

Fewer Hints   More Hints

Hide   Show

that triggers the hint, making it ideal for young people learning to read. Tap the menu icon with the three vertical dots and tap **Word Wise** to set it up or turn it off.

Goodreads: Amazon created yet more buzz in the book industry when it acquired Goodreads and its 20 million members. The Fire lets Goodreads members sync their Fire HD tablet and Goodreads accounts to automatically post their Amazon book purchases to Goodreads. This feature allows sharing of "Want to Read" lists and rapid exchange of reading lists between Goodreads friends.

To access Goodreads, tap Books in the Category Bar, tap Library, and tap the Goodreads button at the top of your library screen, or swipe left to right to display the sidebar menu and tap Goodreads. You will need your Goodreads login and password information to access your account.

Downloading Free Ebooks

The Fire HD has made books more affordable than ever, and free titles are easy to find, both in the Amazon Book Store and on third-party websites. Here are some places to look for free reading material.

Amazon has two special programs that offer free books. The first is Prime Reading. Yes, as well as music, films and TV you also get free ebooks and digital magazines with an Amazon Prime membership. To access Prime Reading, navigate again to the **Books** category screen on your tablet and click on the Store icon.

Once in the Amazon book store you should see a link to Prime Reading towards the middle of the screen, click on it. From there you can browse all the books and magazines that are currently available for free as part of your Prime membership.

The second Amazon free books program is Free Popular Classics. These are older titles in the public domain whose copyright has expired. Thousands of classic works of literature are available for download to your Fire tablet, including Les Misérables, A Tale of Two Cities, Alice in Wonderland, and Jane Eyre. To browse this collection, type free popular classics into the search box on your tablet.

Internet Archive: This nonprofit site has collected over 2.5 million book titles that you can read on your Fire, but you will need to download each ebook to your Mac or PC first. In your computer's browser, go to **archive.org** and search for a title, or scroll down to browse the subcollections. Choose a book, click **Details**, and look in the right sidebar for the Kindle version download link. Save the file to your computer. From your hard drive, you can transfer the file to your Fire using either the micro USB cable, or by emailing it to yourself as an attachment and downloading the book in your Fire's email app. See **Chapter 8** for more file transfer options.

Open Library: This enormous free library contains 1 million free ebook titles, but not all of them are available for the Fire tablet, and some of them require you to register first. From your Mac or PC browser window, go to **openlibrary.org** and click the "1,000,000 free ebook titles" link near the top of the screen. Search for the title you want, or browse by subject, author, or keyword from the menu at the top left. Be sure to choose to choose the *Ebooks* option. Click on a title to see whether you can download it as a MOBI file, or if there's a Send to Kindle Option. If you can, click it to download and transfer it from your hard drive to your Fire as we explain above. For some titles, you can also download a Fire edition directly to your device from the Silk browser.

Project Gutenburg: This free site holds 50,000 titles. Use your Mac or PC to browse to **gutenberg.org** and search for the title you want, or browse by category. When you find a book, click the Kindle with Images link and download it to your hard drive, then transfer it over to your Fire HD using one of the methods explained above.

ManyBooks: This library has 33,000 free ebooks but you have to sign up for a free subscription with your email address. Use your computer to search for a title or browse the categories, then click on a title and use the Download menu on the right to grab the MOBI version so you can transfer it over to your Fire tablet.

Borrowing Books from Amazon

Amazon is more than a bookstore - it also functions as a gigantic lending library. If you have an Amazon Prime membership, then you can borrow books for free, which really is an incredible deal. Without Prime, you will pay a fee to borrow a book. The Lending Library program limits you to one borrow per month, but there are no due dates. Only Kindle e-reader, Fire tablet, and Fire Phone owners are eligible for this program.

To borrow a book on your Fire, tap *Books* in the Category Bar and tap Store. Swipe left to right to display the sidebar menu and tap *Kindle Owners Lending Library* to bring up a list of titles you can borrow for free with Prime. Tap any title to display the book's information page, and tap Borrow for Free. The book will download to your Fire and open for you to read. You can add notes and highlights to a borrowed book just as you can for a book you own, and they will be saved in your account.

The easiest way to return a book is simply to borrow another one. During the borrowing process, you will be prompted to return the old one. Another method is to go to the Amazon home page in the Silk browser and choose Manage Your Fire from the drop-down menu under Your Account. Tap the Actions button next to the title you want to return and follow the prompts. You can also follow the same process on your PC or Mac.

Borrowing Amazon Books Through Your Local Library: Amazon's Overdrive program allows more than 10,000 libraries in the United States to lend Fire titles to their patrons who have Amazon accounts - no Prime membership required! Each library has its own lending policy, but generally there are restrictions on how many ebooks you can borrow at a time, and how long you can check them out. You will also need to set up an account and PIN for the library you are using.

From your Fire's Silk browser or your laptop or desktop computer, use your library's online card catalog to search for ebooks (some libraries call them digital books). Click on the title and click *Get Ebook* or a similar-sounding link. At this point you will need to select your library name and type in your PIN number.

The book and its description will appear in a new screen. Click the *Borrow* button and choose Kindle format from the drop-down menu. Overdrive will now take you to the Amazon website. Click the *Get Library Book* button on the right and download it to your Fire or your computer. If you used your computer for this, you will need to transfer the book's MOBI file to your Fire using the instructions above or in **Chapter 8**.

If the Borrow button has been replaced with a *Place a Hold* button, then you will have to place a hold on the title to read it later - Amazon Overdrive limits the number of copies of any single title that can be checked out in your library system at one time. Unfortunately, if your title is checked out, you will have to backtrack several screens to search for another one, and possibly enter your PIN again.

The advice above is one way to go. Another option is to download the Overdrive Media Console (**www.amazon.com/dp/B00850NK6I**) app which you can download for free from the Amazon app store (use the link or just search for "Overdrive"). Using this app should allow you to do everything necessary to complete the whole process from one place. We haven't used this app and have heard mixed feedback with some Fire users absolutely loving it and other saying that they can't get it to work. Looking at recent reviews suggests that improvement and fixes have been made.

Lending Your Fire Books to a Friend: You can lend items from your Fire Book Library to one person for up to 14 days. The borrower can read it on a Kindle or Fire device, or on a PC or Mac after downloading and installing the Kindle Reader software.

To lend a book, go to the Amazon home page in the Fire Silk browser or your computer browser, and choose **Manage Your Content and Devices** from the drop-down menu under Your Account. Tap the Actions button next to the title you want to lend and choose **Lend This Book**.

Amazon will prompt you for the borrower's password. Click the Send Now button. Note that lending is not available for some Amazon titles, and that each of your books can only be loaned once. You will not be able to read the book while it is out on loan.

Buying and Reading Newsstand Items

The Fire Newsstand is where you can subscribe to magazines, newspapers, and blogs that require a subscription fee. Tap **Newsstand** in the Category Bar and tap **Store**. Under your Newsstand Library items you will see a display of Recommended for You magazine titles and some best sellers.

To start a subscription through 1-Click Ordering, tap any item and tap the **Subscribe Now** button or **Try Free for 30 days**. Newsstand items with interactive features will require a free app for that item, which you can download from the App Store and then activate your subscription with an in-app purchase.

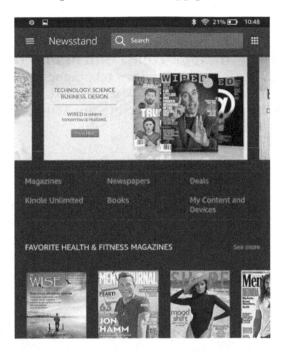

To view your Newsstand items, tap **Newsstand** in the Category Bar and tap **Library.** Fire only keeps the current issue of each Newsstand item on your device. To see up to 12 back issues of any magazine or 14 back issues of any newspaper, tap the title in the All tab of your Library and tap the back issue you want to download to your Fire.

Older back issues can be downloaded from your Subscription Settings page. You can access this page a couple of different ways. The easiest way is to swipe down from the top to open the Quick Settings menu, tap the **Settings** gear icon, tap **My Account**, tap **Amazon Account Settings,** then scroll down and tap **Memberships and Subscriptions**.

Sign in and from there you should see and navigate to the Kindle Newsstand Subscription Manager use the Actions button to deliver past issues to your Fire tablet. If you have purchased a Newsstand item with a free 30-day trial, you can cancel your subscription from this page before Amazon charges your credit card for it.

You can also use the Silk browser or your computer browser to navigate from Amazon's home page to your Amazon account page and finally to your **Manage Your Content and Devices** page. Choose your device from the **Devices** tab. Using the Manage menu on the left, you can download back issues and activate or cancel subscriptions to newsstand items using the Actions button on the right.

6. LISTENING TO MUSIC

Your Fire tablet makes a great music player. We were surprised to find that holding the Fire tablet doesn't interfere with the sound quality, nor does a properly designed protective case made specifically for the Fire (see **Chapter 11**). You can make your Fire sound even better with a good pair of headphones.

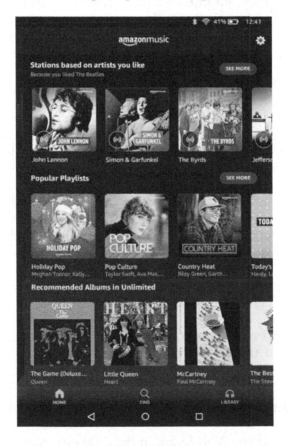

About the Music Packages from Amazon

The Amazon digital music inventory is running at over 40 million songs, so there's something for everyone! However, the music that you will be able to access on your Fire tablet will depend on which of the Amazon music packages you decide to take.

There are basically four options for you to use with your Fire tablet:

- Amazon Music - the basic package that is **free** for all Amazon and Fire tablet customers, and offers thousands of songs and streaming stations (with ads) to listen to online. Note that you cannot listen to music offline on this free package.

- Amazon Music Unlimited – a **paid-for** subscription service that allows you access to the entire catalog, over 40 million songs, thousands of curated playlists and streaming stations, the option of creating your own playlists, listening to music offline and no ads. There are different Amazon Music Unlimited subscription plans (individual, family, single-device etc.) starting from $9.99 per month.

- Prime Music - available as part of your **paid-for** Prime subscription; with over 2 million songs, thousands of curated playlists and streaming stations, the option of creating your own playlists, listening to music offline and no ads. Prime subscriptions start at $12.99 per month and offer a host of benefits, including the Prime Music offer. (Note that Prime members can also get a discounted Amazon Music Unlimited package, if you want to access the full amazon music catalog.)

- You can also simply buy digital albums individually if you prefer not to have a monthly music subscription.

You can see more details about the different options here: **https://amzn.to/2JSToWU**

Accessing Music on the Fire Tablet

When you select the *Music* tab in the Category Bar on your Fire's home screen you'll see two options on the right, *My Music* and *Browse*. If you are already a Prime member and you've already explored the music offer that comes with the Prime package you'll also be able to see your last Prime Music interaction here.

Tap **Browse** to see the options available online via the free Amazon Music package. If you've never used any Amazon music service, the first time you explore the Music category on Fire tablet, you may be asked to choose music genres or artists you like, so that Amazon can offer you a more curated search.

The Browse page will show Top Stations (a station is essentially like a radio station with music streamed of a particular genre, artist or decade) and a few selections of curated Popular Playlists or Playlists for You (based on previous browsing history).

You may also see Recommended Albums in Unlimited. To play those albums you will need to upgrade from the free package to Amazon Unlimited, then at the top of the Browse page you'll see the Amazon Music logo and a gear type icon. Tap on the **gear icon** to go to **Music Settings** and follow the prompts to set up the monthly subscription payment.

Note if you are trying to use other functions within Music and you find your Fire doesn't respond it'll probably be because you only have the free Amazon Music package; and you'll need to upgrade to either Unlimited or Prime Music.

Remember the music that is available on the free Amazon Music package can only be accessed when you're online (another sly Amazon incentive to buy a subscription). If you don't want to buy a subscription then you can simply buy digital music direct from Amazon. On the Browse page, go to the **gear icon** and then select the **Store**.

The Amazon Music Store displays lots of eye-catching photos and graphics to entice you into expanding your listening library. Tap the Store icon to see several rows of recommendations customized for you based on your previous purchase and listening history. To see additional categories, tap one of the tabs at the top of the Store screen to browse by Genres, Best Sellers, or New Releases. You can browse the Music Store using any of these categories. Tap any thumbnail to learn more about the selection. From the selection's information page, you can tap the circled number next to any track to listen to a sample clip.

To search for an album or song, tap the Search box and type an album, song, or artist into it using the Fire tablet's onscreen keyboard or the voice command.

To buy a selection, tap the price button, which will change to say Buy Now. Tapping it again will charge your 1-Click Ordering account for the price of the selection and store it in your Amazon Cloud library. Free music still registers as a sale in your 1-Click Ordering account in the amount of $0.00. A pop-up menu will open and give you the choice of either going to your My Music library and listening to your purchase, or continuing to shop.

As mentioned before, Amazon has sweetened the deal for its Prime members by offering them a huge catalog of 2 million songs, as well as albums, pre-selected Prime Playlists, and stations, absolutely free. You can also create your own playlists by mixing up Prime Music selections with your own musical tracks and saving the result.

If you're a Prime member, you can browse for Prime Music selections by tapping Music in the Category Bar. Tap Browse to access all your free Prime music content, including Recommended, Stations and Playlists. Just tap the + icon to add a Prime Music song to your My Music library for free. You can add an entire playlist by tapping the menu icon with the three vertical dots next to the playlist and tap Add to Library from the pop-up menu.

You can also use the *Search icon* at the bottom of on any page in Browse or My Music to hunt for your favorite song, artist, album, or genre using the keyboard or voice command.

Any Prime Music selections you add to your Music Library display right along with your other songs and albums, no matter how you sort the items (by album, song, artist, or genre). The Prime Playlists section under "Your Playlists" shows the Prime Playlists you've added to your library.

Prime members can listen to their Prime Music selections in their Amazon Cloud library in the cloud on virtually any device they own, as well as directly on Amazon.com. Prime Music can only be downloaded to phones and tablets that support Amazon Music. This app is built into your Fire, but you must download it to other devices, and your Prime Music selections can't be exported to other devices. You must access your downloaded selections while connected to a wireless network every 30 days or they are automatically deleted.

Be aware that Prime Music titles come and go, so if Amazon decides to remove a selection from Prime, you will need to purchase it before you can listen to it again.

AutoRip: Like many music lovers, we still buy music CDs from Amazon. We like the album art and liner notes, and their sound quality is better than MP3 files, but of course you can't play them on a tablet or smartphone without ripping them to MP3 format first. That why we love Amazon's AutoRip service. As soon as your CD order ships, AutoRip automatically puts an MP3 copy into your Amazon Music Library, where you can listen to it from the Cloud tab, or download it to your Fire and play it from the Device tab. Not only that, it automatically adds all of your Amazon CD purchases dating back to 1998 to your Music Library - awesome! There's only one catch: some of your CDs might not be eligible for this service, depending on their copyright terms - boo!

Listening to Music

To listen to music on your Fire, tap *Music* from the Home screen Category Bar; on the top right-hand side of the Music page you'll see icons for My Music (an image of headphones) and an icon to Browse the Amazon Music library (a rectangular shape with two lines above).

To scroll through your personal music collection, tap on My Music to go to a new page where you can choose these different options to find your music: Playlists, Artists, Albums, Songs, or Genres.

Once you're on the option you want, for example Playlists, tap any thumbnail to open and play your selection (we explain how to create playlists later in this chapter.) When you play a song from an album or playlist, your Fire will move to the next song when the first one finishes.

When you press play a pop-up player controls page will appear with a larger icon of the track or album cover, plus player controls. Tap on the appropriate button to pause, skip to the next or previous song, shuffle, or repeat; use the manual volume controls located on the top of your Fire tablet.

Amazon has rolled out a song lyrics feature for selected songs in its Music store. On the player controls page as you play one of these songs on your Fire, you will also see the lyrics displayed on your screen and scroll line by line as the song progresses. Photos and facts about the artist are featured along with song lyrics. More and more songs are becoming available with this feature.

Whenever music is playing, you'll notice a smaller icon of the track at the bottom center of the My Music option pages - this is a mini player control option with the ability to pause or play.

Also worth noting, when you're on any of the My Music option pages (e.g. Playlists, Artists, Albums, Songs, or Genres) at the top of the page you will see a drop-down arrow. Tap on this and choose Online Music to access your online music stored in the Amazon Cloud, or tap Offline Music to access only the music stored on your Fire HD tablet.

You can also select the Settings gear icon at the top of the screen to change how your device handles music storage and downloads, block explicit songs, or set a sleep timer where your music turns off automatically after defined period.

At the bottom of this, and on any of the My Music option pages, you'll see four icons: Browse, Recents (which will show your recent activity in your Music library), My Music (which will be a brighter blue color at this point) and the Search icon.

Listening from your Amazon Cloud Library: Your Fire contains a built-in media player for streaming music through your Fire from your Amazon Cloud library account. (See end of Chapter 1 for more about the cloud.) Your Fire's internal data storage isn't big enough to hold an extensive music library, but your Music Library in the cloud contains your complete collection of Amazon music purchases.

We have found that it's more convenient to store our music in the cloud and stream it, even though it uses somewhat more battery life.

If you do want to download music to your device for offline listening we recommend you buy a memory card to increase your storage space. Your Fire HD 8's storage can be expanded to take 1TB!

To stream music stored in your Music Library, tap Music from the Home screen Category Bar and tap My Music. Tap the icon for any selection to start listening. At the top of the page next to the gear icon you can tap and switch between Online Music and Offline Music

Listening Offline: If you are traveling to a location with no Wi-Fi access, then storing as much music as you can fit on your device will be a better option.

To download music from the cloud, open your Music Library from the Category Bar, tap My Music. Make sure your tablet is currently showing Online Music. Find your selection on the list, tap the menu icon with the three vertical dots, and tap Download from the pop-up menu.

To remove a selection from your Fire, tap Remove from Device from the same pop-up menu. This takes the item off your Fire but leaves it in your cloud Music Library to download again at any time. Remember, don't delete any purchased music from your Amazon Cloud library, or you will have to buy it again to listen to it!

Managing Your Music Library

Creating Playlists: You can create your own playlists in your Amazon music library by adding the songs and albums you've stored in the cloud or on your Fire tablet. Tap the menu icon with the three vertical dots next to any selection and tap Add to Playlist in the pop-up menu. Add it to an existing playlist by tapping that list, or tap Create New Playlist. Give it a name and tap Save to add your selection to the new list. If the app does not offer the Add Playlist option, then you may need to upgrade to a Prime Music or Amazon Music Unlimited subscription.

To delete an item from a playlist, select the playlist you want to delete the selection from and tap the menu icon next to that selection. Tap Remove from Playlist in the pop-up menu to delete the item.

Prime Playlists and Stations: If you're an Amazon Prime member, check out the selection of pre-populated playlists and Stations available for free. From the Category Bar on the Home screen tap Music and tap Browse. Tap Playlists or Stations to bring up compilations like "Pop to Make You Feel Better" and "Singing in the Shower," as well as more conventional classic rock and techno lists. Lengths vary from 90 minutes to over3 hours so you can tap a list and forget about it while it plays.

Even better, add any Playlist to your music library, again tap the three dots to the right of any playlist and tap Add to My Music or Download to have it right there on your device for offline listening.

Buying and Listening to Audiobooks with Audible

Audiobooks have their own library that you can access from the Category Bar on the Home screen of your Fire tablet, under *Audible*.

Tap *Store* to shop for audiobooks on Amazon. Shopping for and managing this library is very similar to buying and managing ebooks in your Books Library (see **Chapter 5**). The Audiobooks shopping menu has a Wish List option, and it downloads your purchases automatically through your 1-Click Shopping account.

Titles you purchase are added to the your Audiobooks library, where you can call up a list of your titles by tapping *Library*. Tap *All* to display your audiobooks stored in your Amazon Cloud library, or tap *Downloaded* to display titles stored on your device.

Keep in mind that audiobooks take up a lot of storage space on your device. To shop by category, tap **Store** from the Audiobooks content category, swipe left to right to display the sidebar menu, and tap ***Browse Categories***.

The Fire's built-in audiobook player displays a control panel where you can adjust its reading speed to slower or faster than normal, add bookmarks, pause the audio, back up 30 seconds, and adjust the playback volume. The player control panel also has a Sleep function that we really love. You can actually set your Fire to read you to sleep at night for 15 to 60 minutes, or to the end of a chapter - lovely!

You can add a note when you place a bookmark by tapping and holding the ***Bookmark key*** until the onscreen keyboard pops up.

To display your list of bookmarks, tap the small notebook icon in the upper right corner while the audiobook is open in the player. Tap and hold any bookmark to edit your notes or delete the bookmark. Swiping left to right will display the sidebar menu with lots of options for managing your audiobook library and player. The sidebar menu also contains options for jumping from chapter to chapter and details about each audiobook title.

Although Amazon audiobooks aren't part of the Lending Library program for Prime members, we found that our local library loans out selected audiobook titles through Amazon's Overdrive program (see **Chapter 5**).

Audible: If you don't already have an Audible account subscription, then you'll be encouraged to get one when you first go into the audiobooks **Store**. If you enjoy audiobooks, and plan to listen to at least one a month, then getting an Audible account makes sense as the monthly fee is often much lower than buying an audio book as a one-off.

To find out more you can go to **Audible.com** and sign up for a 30-day trial, you get a free audiobook to add to your library before the monthly subscription fee kicks in.

There's also an Audible app for Android that's free to download from the Amazon App Store and offers some great features if you opt for the monthly subscription plan as an in-app purchase. Audible is an Amazon company, so their website sells the entire library of Amazon ebooks and audiobooks for you to read or listen to on your Fire tablet.

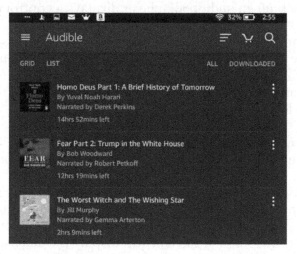

You can purchase your Audible subscription via your Fire tablet, from the Amazon App store or from your Mac or PC. The cheapest plan gives you one free audiobook per month plus discounts on additional audiobook purchases, while the expanded plans cost more but give you more free audiobook downloads. As mentioned, we listen to a lot of audiobooks, and they aren't cheap to purchase, so this subscription plan has been worthwhile for us, and with over 180,000 audiobooks to choose from, we haven't run out of material yet.

Check out Audible's Immersion Reading feature, which highlights each word of your audiobook in the text version as the word is spoken. Audible also manages Amazon's Whispersync function, which saves the highlights and bookmarks you place in your Fire ebook library and syncs them across all of your devices.

And you can also set the Audible app to be Button-Free - opening your user experience to a more fluid interaction with the use of some neat shortcuts. For example, once your book is playing through the Audible app, you need only tap anywhere on the Fire

HD screen to pause or play, swipe left or right to go backwards and forwards, swipe down to skip a chapter, and tap and hold the screen to create a bookmark.

7. WATCHING MOVIES

With its high-resolution display and excellent audio quality, the Fire HD might be the ultimate portable video player. Amazon's Prime Video store has over 150,000 titles, and the Fire's portable size lets you take your movie watching anywhere you go. Note that you do not need a Prime subscription to shop in the video store (we'll cover how, below).

Amazon has also developed its exclusive Advance Streaming and Prediction (ASAP) technology to address a common customer complaint about Internet video streaming: buffering.

You've probably experienced stuttering, "hanging," and audio out of sync with the video when you play videos through your computer's web browser, and possibly with other digital media players you've tried out.

Buffering occurs because most people's broadband service isn't up to the heavy bandwidth usage demands of digital media streaming.

Amazon's solution is to tap into your user history and use it to predict which movies and TV episodes you might want to watch.

These titles are preloaded into your account on their server. If you buy or rent one of these titles, they're already buffered for you and waiting for instant playback – A-S-A-P.

Buying or Renting Videos from Amazon

To shop in the Prime Video store, tap **Video** in the Category Bar on your Fire's home screen. On the right-hand side you'll see the **Prime Video** icon, tap this to go video shopping (don't worry, doing this does not tie you into a prime subscription). You'll also see on the main Video category page a **Downloaded** icon.

Now that you're in the Prime Video store you can browse the various categories, or at the bottom of the page you'll see a Search icon where you can look for something in particular. You can also use voice command to search the Prime Video store.

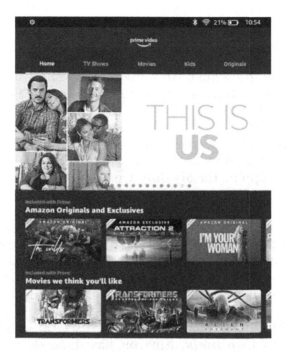

You'll note that many of the movies or TV series available will be listed as **Included with Prime** or have the Prime logo on the top left of their image: these movies and series are only available to watch if you have a Prime subscription.

Movies or series that do not have the Prime logo are available either to **Buy** outright (usually for around $10) or to **Rent** (usually about $4). Clicking one of these buttons will charge your 1-Click Ordering account so you can get the video. You can choose to start watching it right away, or save it in your Video Library.

Note that the first options for sale or rent will be the highest-definition version of the movie - currently ultra-high definition (UHD). The Fire tablet does not support UHD yet, but will play a UHD movie in the highest supported resolution of the device. However, here's a teeny money-saving tip - if you look carefully at the sales page of your selected movie you'll see the words **More**

Purchase Options in blue. Tap this to buy or rent the movie at a lower price and in a lower HD or SD resolution! Every dollar counts, right?!

If you want to go straight to the non Prime video options, then tap on the **Store** icon at the bottom of the Prime Video page, where you'll then be presented with many different lists of movies available to rent or buy, or you can search using the Search icon or voice command.

Once you purchase or rent the video, it will appear in your Downloaded list back on the first page of the Video category, or you can find it by tapping the My Stuff icon at the bottom of the Video Store page.

Rented titles will stay in your video library for 30-days from the date of the rental. However, once you press play on the rented title, you have at minimum 48-hours to watch it. There is no need to return a rental video - it simply becomes unavailable when you tap it in your Video Library until you rent it again or buy it.

Browsing the Video store, you'll also see a selection titled **Subscribe to Channels**. Amazon has done clever deals with various cable TV channels (such as HBO, Showtime, Hallmark Movies, PBS Kids, Comedy Central, and more), so that Prime members can have a reduced subscription to these channels. This effectively allows you the "cut the cord" with traditional cable TV subscriptions, whilst still enjoying the full video offering of those cable channels. Each cable network charges their own reduced rate for Prime members.

To use the X-Ray feature to learn more about a video, tap its thumbnail in the Video Store and then More Details to see a rich selection of facts and trivia from the Internet Movie Database (IMDb), which is also available for free as an app in the Amazon App Store.

Most Video Store movies will have a Watch Trailer button under the thumbnail so you can see the preview. TV shows will list which seasons are available and their prices.
Tap on the My Stuff icon at the bottom of the Prime Video page, to

see your Downloads, Purchases and your Watch List. You can add videos you have purchased and videos you want to save for possible purchase later to this list. To scroll through the Watch List, swipe down the display of thumbnails. To mark a video in the Store to return to later, tap the Add to Watchlist button for that item.

Amazon Prime Video: We've mentioned this above a few times, but just to be clear. There are now thousands of videos in the Amazon store that are available to Prime members for free - yes, you read that right! All Prime Video media can be streamed to your Fire through your Wi-Fi connection, and Amazon now offers over half of this collection for downloading as well, and there are special Prime member subscriptions available for cable TV channels that are also available to stream onto your tablet. Just one more excellent reason to buy a Prime membership.

Watching Videos

By default, all of your purchases from the Video Store are streamed to you via your Wi-Fi connection to save data storage space on your Fire tablet. Streaming requires you to be in an area with an active Wi-Fi connection, and remember that it uses up some battery juice on your device. To watch a video, tap the item in the Store or in your Watchlist and then tap Watch Now.

Video Player Controls: To display the video player control panel, simply tap the screen while you are watching a video. You have to tap pause to access the speaker icon to bring up the volume slider and the slider allows you to turn the volume up or down. The pause button lets you pause or resume the video when you tap it. There is also a 10-second skip back button and a 10-second skip forward button. Finally, the video scrub bar lets you move forward or backward in slow motion through the video to a frame of your choice by dragging your finger across the bar.

Watching Downloaded Videos: If you want to watch a video in a location with no Wi-Fi connection, then you will need to download it to your Fire tablet first. Tap the video's thumbnail in the Video

Store or the Watch List and tap Download to save the video to your Fire. The menu will give you the choice of downloading the video in HD or SD format, and your answer will depend on how much storage space is left on your device and how important HD resolution is to you for this particular video.

If you want to pause or cancel the download, tap the Download Options button and tap Cancel Download.

To view the downloaded video from your Fire without a Wi-Fi connection, tap the video's thumbnail and then tap Watch Now. Remember that some Prime Instant Video selections are not available for download.

If you want to find out more about Amazon Prime our other book - **Amazon Prime & Kindle Unlimited: Newbie to Expert in 1 Hour! (www.amazon.com/dp/Bo8PSDN28D)** - has more info.

Streaming from Third-Party Sites

Alongside all the content from Prime Video, third-party video streaming services like Netflix, Hulu, Sling, Disney+, Philo, HBO GO and NOW, Starz, DC Universe and Showtime are also available on your Fire tablet.

You can set up these TV provider services either via the Prime Video channel subscriptions (see above) or by the specific providers app which you can download for free from the Amazon App Store (see **Chapter 4**). Note, however, that whilst these apps are free, you will still need to have an account with the TV provider in question.

Free video streaming sites such as YouTube and Vimeo have one issue with the Fire, and that is the Silk browser's lack of support for Flash video. Both of these video sharing sites are moving toward HTML5 as they phase out Flash, so this situation should continue to improve.

8. WORKING WITH PHOTOS AND DOCUMENTS

With its front-facing and rear-facing cameras, the Fire tablet has joined the ranks of bona fide tablets such as the far more expensive Apple and Samsung products.

You can take photos, videos, and self-portraits, and the built-in microphone makes Skype calls and video chat a reality.

Taking Photos with the Fire HD

To use the Fire HD's built-in cameras, tap the **Camera app** in the in the Apps Grid. When the app opens, tap the double arrow icon to toggle back and forth between the two cameras on your tablet.

The front-facing camera faces toward you, while the rear-facing camera faces away from you.

To take a photo, tap the shutter icon 🌀. Your image will be automatically saved, but Film Strip 📷 displays recent photos in a strip across the lower edge of your screen.

Tap the **Film Strip** icon to toggle between displaying and hiding the Film Strip. To delete a photo from your Fire, tap the image in the Film Strip or on the touchscreen display and tap the bin icon then tap **Delete**.

To display the Camera Settings while the Camera app is open, tap the gear icon ⚙ in the upper right corner of the screen and use the toggle sliders to activate or deactivate the app's features.

This menu allows you to activate or deactivate HDR (High Dynamic Range) for the rear-facing camera only, which will give you better photo quality in low light or shadowy settings.

You can also activate the **Image Review** feature which

temporarily displays each photo you take so you can decide whether to keep or delete it.

The Settings Menu also controls panorama, and lenticular (rapid-fire camera shots).

To hide the **Settings** menu, tap the gear icon again.

When you tap on any image in the camera roll, as well as the bin icon for deleting photos, the Share icon in the Camera Roll lets you share the image via email, a Bluetooth device, Facebook, Skype or Twitter. The pencil icon offers some nice editing features for retouching and optimizing your photos right on your Fire HD tablet.

Taking Videos: The rear-facing camera records videos with sound. Open the Camera app and tap the red video icon to start recording.

You can zoom in and out by pinching the screen with two fingers, or by using the volume buttons on the edge of your tablet's case. Tap the video icon again to stop recording and store or delete the video.

Taking Panoramic Photos: The rear-facing camera takes long photos in either a horizontal or vertical direction. Activate the Camera app from the App Grid.

Open the Camera app and tap the gear icon, then tap **Panorama**.

Tap the blue capture icon and move your Fire tablet slowly in the direction you would like to capture the panoramic photo, or touch and slide the arrow in the preview strip.

Tap the white square inside the blue capture icon to save.

Photos App

As mentioned, when you take a photo it is automatically saved and you can see your most recently saved photos in the Camera Roll strip across the bottom of the screen when your camera app is open.

So where have your photos been saved to? The answer is your Photos app which looks like this:

All Amazon account holders get 5GB of cloud storage for their photos and videos, while Prime members get unlimited photo storage for photos taken on their Fire tablet.

Annoyingly, there is no quick link between your camera and the rest of your photos in the Photo app. You'll need to exit the camera app and return to your Home screen and open the Photo app.

When viewing the Photo app you will see your options across the bottom of the screen. From left to right you will see

Yours - Your photos

Family - This is your family vault, invite other members of your family to share their photos to your Photo app

Albums - create albums where you keep photos in groups

More - Here are other ways of viewing your photos and your Settings

When viewing a photo in the Photo app you can tap the three dots in the top right-hand corner and give yourself the option to delete, edit or hide the photo. You can also add the photo to an album, download it to your tablet (rather than just storing it in the cloud), make the image part of a slideshow or set it as a wallpaper for your tablet.

Transferring Photo and Document Files

For transferring an occasional photo or document file between your Fire and another device, an attachment sent through your regular email account works fine. For sharing photo albums and other multiple file collections, you will need something more heavy duty. Here are three ways to transfer data between other devices and your Fire HD tablet.

USB Transfer: To transfer files between your Fire HD tablet and a computer, plug the full-size end of the micro USB cable into a USB 2.0 port on your computer, and plug the micro end of the cable into your Fire. Mac users should install Android's free File Transfer app on their computer first, from **www.android.com/filetransfer/**.

Once connected, your Fire HD will display as an external drive icon in your computer's file directory. Click it open, then click the Internal Storage folder, and then the Documents folder to display the files on your Fire's storage drive.

On your computer's hard drive, find the file you want to transfer and simply drag and drop it to the Fire's Documents folder. Eject the Fire device icon from your desktop before unplugging the USB cable.

The Fire should automatically detect the type of file you have transferred and will put it in the correct content library. When you open that library, the transferred file will show up under the Device tab. It won't show up in the Cloud tab because the Fire tablet doesn't back up USB transfers to the cloud.

You can also drag and drop files from your Fire tablet to your computer's hard drive with a USB connection. These files can then be transferred to another Kindle or Fire device, or to a smartphone.

Personal Documents Service: This Amazon service lets you send multiple files and large files between your Fire and another device. Unlike a USB transfer, this method stores your data files safely in the Amazon Cloud where you can retrieve them at any time. There is no charge to use this service over Wi-Fi.

Your Fire assigns you a unique email address for using the Personal Documents Service. To find it, tap the Docs app icon in the Apps Grid and swipe left to right. Tap **Settings** and you should see an email address that ends with @kindle.com ...jot it down.

Before anyone can send documents to your Amazon email address, you need to pre-approve their email address. Go to your Amazon account via your PC or Mac and choose **Manage Your Content and Devices**, then click the Preferences tab at the right and scroll down to **Personal Document Settings**. You can then enter the sender's address under Approved Personal Document E-mail List by clicking **Add a New Approved Email Address**. You should also add any of your own email accounts that you plan to use for this service.

Approved senders can send you up to 25 attached documents per email, with the size of each document limited to 50MB before zipping. You must receive and open the email with the Fire email app within 60 days to avoid deletion. Personal Documents Service will store the attachments in your Amazon Cloud library, where you can download them to your Fire HD at any time with the Docs app in the App Grid. The Docs app organizes your documents into folders, which you open by tapping. Download a single file by tapping its icon, or download multiple files by tapping **Select All** in the upper right corner of the Docs screen and tapping the items you want to download.

You or another sender can speed up the document attachment process on their end by downloading and installing the Send to Kindle application to their computer or Android device. Amazon makes versions of Send to Kindle for PCs, Macs, Android, and specific web browsers. Go to **www.amazon.com/sendtokindle** to download it for your device.

Amazon Drive: For really heavy-duty uploading, you can install the Amazon Photo desktop application on your computer and upload up to 2GB of data at a time directly to your Amazon Drive Library account (storage space permitting), where it's available for viewing or downloading.

To install Amazon Photo desktop application on your computer, go to **www.amazon.com/photos/download** and let the site automatically detect which version you need before it presents you with a download. You can also click *Your Amazon Drive* from the drop-down menu under *Your Account* on the Amazon home screen and install the application from there. Open and install the downloaded file to your hard drive. This application will then let you connect to your Amazon Drive with your computer so you can upload and download data with a simple drag-and-drop interface.

Alternatively, you can just upload your documents, photos and videos straight into your Amazon Drive account via your web browser. Go to the main Amazon Drive page (**www.amazon.com/clouddrive**) and click on the *Upload* tab located at the top left of the page. You can then choose to upload a folder or individual files and browse your computer for the relevant content you wish to store.

Working with Documents

Office Suite: The Docs app in your Fire App Grid has some of the same functionality of Microsoft Office. Open the app and tap the + *icon* in the upper right corner of your screen. In the Create pop-up menu, tap *Document*, *Spreadsheet*, or *Presentation* to create a document to save. There are also several office suite apps for the Fire available in the App Store. Amazon Underground features a free office app called OfficeSuite Pro.

Wireless Printing: The Fire HD tablet has a robust wireless printing option. From the WPS Office app, your Photo Library, or the Fire email app you can send documents, spreadsheets, emails, images, and presentations to any printer connected to a wi-fi network. The Fire auto-detects all available printers in your network.

Business Productivity: The Fire can be set up to log in to your company's intranet, even if it's set up with Microsoft Exchange. You can the great selection of office productivity apps for the Fire to submit timesheets, expense reports, share and edit documents, and sync your email, contacts, and calendar. Remote VPN access with full encryption is also available from the Settings menu for even greater connectivity and security.

Creating Folders

We like the free app ES File Explorer File Manager (**www.amazon.com/dp/B008K6HN8I**) for both creating and managing folders on our Fire tablet. This nifty little app gives your tablet's storage drive full Windows-like functionality. You can create new folders, select multiple files or folders, drag and drop files and folders, rename them, and - if you dare - delete them. The app also creates shortcuts and has a really well devised search function that sorts by name, date, file size, or category. To install it on your Fire, tap **Apps** in the Category Bar and tap **Store** to go to the App store, where you can use the search box or voice command to find it and download it.

Other Useful Image/Document Functions

Sending PDFs: In order to send a PDF document, you will first need to convert it to the AZW format for the Fire HD. But this is simplicity itself as your Fire tablet has a built in converter tool - all you have to do is type the word "convert" into your email's subject line, then attach the PDF and send the message to your Amazon email address (see above).

Taking Screenshots: To capture a screenshot from your Fire at any time, place your fingers on the outside edge of your device and press and hold the **Power** button and the **volume-down** part of the Volume button at the same time. If you press them both at the exact same time, your Fire tablet will make a shutter clicking sound, fire off a screenshot and save it in your Photos content library. To go to the album, open the **Photos app** in the App Grid.

Saving web images: Tap and hold the web image and an options box will pop up; simply choose **Download Image** and the image will be saved onto your Fire HD tablet.

Sending multiple images: First tap *Photos* in the App Grid to open your Camera Roll. Tap the checkbox icon in the upper right corner next to the camera icon. Select all the images you want to send by tapping on each image. Tap the *Sharing icon* next to the trash can icon. Finally tap the *Email* button to attach all of them to your email. If you want to send a single image, simply tap and hold it, then choose Email from the list of options. You can also use this screen to share your images on Twitter and Facebook, or to a Bluetooth device.

9. SO WHO AND WHAT IS ALEXA?

As of December 2016 Amazon have updated the software on their Fire tablets and introduced Alexa their voice activated assistant.

Anyone who already owns an Amazon Echo, Echo Show, Echo Dot or Fire TV should already be familiar with Alexa. For those of you who haven't you're in for a treat.

Alexa is the voice activated, computerized personal assistant originally developed for the Amazon Echo Bluetooth speaker. Basically, it is Amazon's answer to Apple's Siri, ask Alexa a question or set her/it a task and Alexa will respond in "her" soft friendly voice.

Alexa is the selling point of the Amazon Echo, without Alexa the Echo is just a Bluetooth speaker and there are plenty of those on the market already.

Amazon is selling the Echo as a device that they hope will become an integral part of your Smart Home.

If you decide to buy an Amazon Echo don't forget to check out our user guide to get the most from your new device:
Amazon Echo User Guide: Newbie to Expert in 1 Hour! (www.amzn.to/3gICaFS)

So how does it work? As discussed in the **Getting Started chapter** there are two ways to operate Alexa with your Fire tablet. You have the option of hands-free control where you say *"Alexa..."* followed by a command.

Alternatively, you can swipe down the quick settings tab and tap the Alexa Hands-free icon to turn hands-free off. Then instead, when you want to interact with Alexa, hold down the Home button (the circle icon at the bottom of the screen) for one second until a blue line illuminates across the bottom of the screen areas.

Now just ask Alexa to perform any number of tasks automatically for you. When you activate Alexa this way you don't need to say the wake word ("Alexa"). The things you can ask for can be broken down into the following categories...

1. Speed up access to other features on your tablet. So, ask Alexa to play a song or audiobook that you've purchased or open a favorite app.

2. Ask questions and get information. So, weather updates, general knowledge questions, sports scores, traffic reports can all be accessed via voice.

3. Increase productivity. Alexa can give you voice access to your calendars and to do lists as well as the ability to set alarms and timers

4. Control smart devices. Lights, thermostats and garage doors are just a few of the smart home devices currently on to the market. You can link Alexa to these products and control them with your voice.

We're going to go into more detail on these features now, but as updates are coming thick and fast for Alexa we also advise you to start by opening the Alexa app, which you should see on your home screen, to get an overview of what you can do. Once the app is opened and you have logged in with your Amazon username and password you should see Things to Try in the left hand menu, this will show you the latest new features.

Below is a precis of the features you will find within the Alexa app. We've written a whole book on Alexa which you can find here - **Alexa: Alexa Skills, Tips & Tricks**
(www.amazon.com/dp/B07BBQHD9Z)

Yes, there really is that much to discover, but what follows should get you started in the right direction...

Music, Radio, Audio and Alexa

Alexa brings you a lot of music options and Alexa can help you control these options using just your voice.

Any music that you have bought via Amazon will be in your music library within the music section of the Alexa app and you can get any track or album playing by saying *"Alexa, play"* followed by the artists name, album or track name.

Going beyond your own personal music collection you can also control music from other sources. Pandora, Tunein and iHeartRadio are just a few of the Internet radio providers offering access to both curated playlists of music and actual radio stations around the world.

Once you have discovered content that you like from these sources all three can be controlled with Alexa. Again, just say *"Alexa, play"* followed by the content you want to hear, for example *"Alexa, play iHeart 90's Radio"* to start iHeartradio's selection of hits from the 90's.

Clearly to get the most out of this feature you need to be quite familiar with the content on offer from these providers so take some time to familiarize yourself with what they offer.

Do you buy and listen to audio books from Audible? If you do just say *"Alexa, Play..."* or *"Alexa, Read..."* followed by the book title that you would like to listen to and you audio book will start.

While you have music or audio playing you can also speak other commands like *"Next song/previous song"*, *"Pause"*, *"Resume"*, *"Stop"* to control your music.

At this time you are unable to adjust the volume using your voice or fast-forward and rewind part of a track.

General Knowledge

Alexa connects to the Cloud and its vast storehouse of data for measurements, conversions, capital cities, times around the world, mountain heights, population numbers, spelling and pronunciation, etc. Ask a question in these categories, and more than likely, you will receive an accurate answer.

Alexa is excellent with trivia too. For simple answers, ask Alexa about people, dates, stars of movies or their dates of release, Academy Award winners by year and category, singers, lyricists, song and album release dates, World Series and Super Bowl winners and much more. Our guess is that you'll enjoy picking Alexa's brain to discover her fountain of interesting factoids about your favorite topics.

So, ask, *"Alexa, who starred in 'To Kill a Mockingbird'?"* and you'll get a list starting with Gregory Peck.

When you want a longer answer, for example, about Gregory Peck, say, *"Alexa, Wikipedia, Gregory Peck."* And the device will read the first paragraph of the Wikipedia entry.

In the category of education, Alexa will be of help with spelling, definitions, conversions, simple calculations, geography, nutritional information and much more that you'll enjoy discovering.

Sports

For sports information from your personal assistant get information
by asking Alexa specific questions such as, *"Alexa...*

- *What is the score of the Dallas Cowboys game?*

- *How are the Boston Red Sox doing?*

- *Who won the Kentucky Wildcats game?*

- *When does the Atlanta Dream play next?*

- *What time do the Los Angeles Dodgers play tomorrow?*

At the time of writing, the Alexa offers scores from the NFL, NBA,WNBA, MLB, MLS, NHL, PGA and NCAA Men's Basketball.

The Amazon Echo is able to access a hit-and-miss blend of other sports information. Questions it could answer when we experimented where:

- *Who won the British Open?*

- *Who won the Belmont Stakes?*

We got, "Sorry, I didn't understand the question I heard" when asking:

- *Who won the NASCAR race?*

- *Who won the Toledo Mudhens game?*

So, you'll have to ask Alexa if she's a fan of your favorite obscure sport or team!

Weather, Traffic and More

Weather information can be accessed by asking these questions or queries similar to them. *"Alexa...*

- *What's the weather for this weekend?"*

- *What's the weather for Tuesday?"*

- *What's the extended forecast?"*

- *What's the weather for next week?"*

- *What's the weather in Chicago?"*

- *Will it rain tomorrow?"*

- *Will it rain in Los Angeles tomorrow?"*

When asked for an extended forecast or the week's weather, Alexa will provide seven days of weather forecast information.

For traffic information you will need the Alexa app. First go to settings within the app and then the Traffic tab. There, you can enter the address of the starting and ending points of your daily commute or a trip you're planning. Additional stops in between can be added and deleted using the buttons.

When you've added these details, ask a question similar to one of these: *"Alexa...*

- *How is traffic?*

- *What's my commute?*

- *What's traffic like?*

Traffic information is provided by HERE, a company owned by Nokia. Alexa gives you the best route to take given current conditions including volume of traffic and construction. The expected time of your commute is given too.

To-Do and Shopping Lists

Like us, you might soon find these Alexa features indispensable. They are certainly easy to use with either voice commands or with the Alexa app. Both your Shopping List and To-do List are featured on the home page of the Alexa app. Choose the one you want to manually add items or activities to.

For the To-do list, use the Add Item box on the Alexa app to populate the list. When you complete a task, select the box next to it, and a check mark will appear and the task will be lined through. Finished tasks are moved to the Completed list while the rest remain on the Active list.

Move back and forth between these lists with the tab at the top of the page. Print the list using the tab at the top. The printer dialogue box will appear for you to use to complete the process.

Or you can just populate the list via voice commands, though it might get a word wrong here or there. We asked, *"Alexa, add 'find CDs' to my to-do list,"* and what appeared on the list was, "Find c.d.s." Later, a note to get "screen grabs" was listed as "screen grahams." Misunderstandings happen most often with uncommon words.

There have been occasions where we've had to think a bit to remember what it was we asked Alexa to add because what's on the list doesn't make sense. It's inspired a blend of comedy, frustration and "ah-ha!" moments when we figure it out.

Typically, a request such as, *"Alexa, add mow the grass to the to-do list"* is clearly understood. Amazon suggests as an alternate saying something like, *"Alexa, I need to organize my tools."* We've found that Alexa doesn't comprehend this voice command very well. We stick to the "Add to to-do list" commands for best results.

Note that checking completed tasks or deleting tasks cannot be done with voice commands; the app must be used. However, you can ask the device something like *"Alexa, what is on my to-do list"* or *"Alexa, read me my to-do list,"* and your request will be granted.

Using the Shopping list function is very similar to creating and managing a to-do list:

- Create it with voice commands or manually using the app

- Ask Alexa to read the list to you for review

- Delete an item you no longer want

- Items must be manually removed; voice recognition won't work for this function

As we said earlier, these features are just the tip of the iceberg and Alexa is changing and growing all the time.

10. TROUBLESHOOTING

What to Do If Your Fire Tablet Freezes

If your Fire touchscreen completely freezes so you can't force-quit a troublesome app (see **Chapter 4**), then it's time for a hard reset. This should be done without the power adapter or USB cable plugged into the device. Press and hold the Power button for 20 seconds before releasing it, then restart.

If you still experience problems, you can try charging the battery through the USB cable and adapter, unplug, and then do another hard reset followed by a restart.

If a hard reset doesn't solve the problem, go here - **www.amzn.to/37cYN29** - on your computer for support.

Lost Passwords or Passcodes

If you lose the password/passcode to either your **Lock Screen** or your **Parental Controls** they can both be reset the same way.

Firstly to reset your Lock Screen password or PIN, enter the wrong passcode five times. After the fifth time (the maximum number of times you are allowed to get it wrong in one session) you will be presented with some different options. Choose **Reset Your PIN** and you will be prompted to enter your main Amazon password (the one you used to register your device and you use to login into Amazon). Once you've done this you will be allowed to select and set a new passcode/password.

For your Parental Control passcode, again enter a wrong passcode five times and after the fifth attempt choose the **Reset Your Parental Controls Passcode** option and, when prompted, enter you main Amazon password. Then set a new passcode and click **Finish**.

Managing Fire HD Updates

It's worth remembering that once you've downloaded an app or ebook, you usually have also allowed the developer to send you updated versions. Updates often allow for smoother running of an app, or improved content. These updates are usually automatic and show up in your notifications but from time to time, you might also want to manually check for any updates via the Manage Your Content and Devices (**www.amazon.com/myk**) website. If there are any updates available for either your apps or books you should see a notification next to the title of the product.

Preserving Battery Life

There are a number of useful steps you can take to help conserve the battery life of your Fire, some of which will really depend on how you use it (see our list below). But almost everyone should consider doing the following as a matter of course.

Firstly, when you're not using your Fire, but don't necessarily want to turn it completely off, you should use the Sleep Mode option to avoid using up battery power. To activate Sleep Mode, touch the **Power** button: the Fire screen should go black immediately without offering up any command options.

If you press the Power button for too long, a message will pop up asking you if you want to shut down - press **Cancel** if the answer is no! To "wake up" your Fire, simply touch the **Power** button again.

You can also choose to set your Fire so that it automatically goes into Sleep Mode after a certain time period of inactivity. Go to *Settings* from the Quick Settings menu or the App Grid, then choose **Power**; here tap on the **Display Settings** option to choose the time delay you want before the Fire goes into Sleep Mode. Click back to your **Power** settings and you can also make sure that **Automatic Smart Suspend** is activated by tapping it so the switch icon displays orange. This disconnects your Fire from all wireless networks if the device is inactive for more than a few minutes.

You can also make sure that apps you're not using are not actually still running - sometimes apps don't fully switch off. Check to see which ones are still running by tapping **Settings** from the Quick Settings menu or the Apps Grid and then **Apps & Games**. Tap **Manage All Applications** and tap **Running** toward the top right of your screen and tap each app to see its status.

An app that has the Force Stop button grayed out is not running, but if isn't grayed out, you can tap it to force quit the app. Use the **Uninstall** button if all else fails, since the app will still be available in your Amazon Cloud library.

At the bottom of each app's management screen you'll see the app's permissions on your Fire. Some of these can be quite intrusive, while others prevent your Fire from sleeping so you'll have to charge your battery more often. It's a good idea to know what your apps are doing while you're asleep!

Some other things you can do to prolong the Fire's battery charge include:

1. Using headphones to listen to audio instead of the speakers

2. Turning down screen brightness

3. Turning off the Automatic Brightness option

4. Disabling Wi-Fi and Bluetooth when you aren't using them

5. Avoiding weak Wi-Fi signals as the Fire has to work harder to stay connected

6. Disabling Location-Based Services in the Settings.

7. Checking for email messages less often

8. Opting for Airplane Mode - but remember that this will mean disabling online access

Troubleshooting Wi-Fi Connections

Wi-Fi connection problems can interfere with data transfers and video streaming, or they can cut you off completely. Sometimes they occur if you don't enter the correct password, or if the network is running MAC filtering. MAC-filtered networks require the network administrator to manually add you as a user before you can use their Wi-Fi connection.

A bad Wi-Fi network connection can also be caused by too many users at once, or connectivity problems from the Fire side. Try putting your device to sleep while the power is on by briefly touching the Power button and touching it again to wake it up. You will need to slide the lock button upward on the touchscreen and enter your password or PIN. This process stops and starts the network connection. If this doesn't work, try restarting your Fire.

We have found that different types of Wi-Fi networks work better with the Fire than others. If you just can't connect, try using your computer's Wi-Fi utility to see whether your network is a WPA2 type as we've found that it's the friendliest for connecting to your Fire.

Traveling Overseas with Your Fire

The most important thing to be aware of when traveling outside the United States with your Fire is that many other countries use 220 volt electrical current instead of the 110 volt used in the US. Be sure to purchase a specialized power adapter or quick charger to handle this.

You will want to travel with your power adapter and USB cable, because you probably won't have access to a computer with a USB connection long enough to handle the longer charging times.

Wi-Fi access can be sporadic when you travel, so plan to download all the content you will need onto your Fire's storage drive before you leave home.

Extended Warranties

Your new Fire tablet comes with a one-year warranty as a standard feature. If you tap **Shop** in the Category Bar and go to the Kindle store on the Amazon website, you can find some extended warranty options for the Fire serviced by third-party providers. A typical plan provides coverage for 2 years against things like accidents and mechanical or electrical failure. Check whether the warranty includes sending you a replacement Fire immediately after you make a claim, with no deductible or shipping fee, and whether the warranty is transferable.

Where to Go for More Help

Amazon's in-house Fire Help Home Page is located at **www.amazon.com/kindlesupport**, or you can open the Help app from the App Grid. From here you can access one-on-one tech support via phone, e-mail, or chat, or you can read a written user guide and view help videos and tutorials.

Several Kindle Fire and Fire forums are available on the web that you can access from your browser. Don't believe everything you read in Internet forums, but sometimes they contain hidden gems for troubleshooting your Fire that you can't find anywhere else. Here are some forums that we have found helpful:

Amazon Customer Forums (**www.amazonforum.com**)

Kindle Boards (**www.kboards.com**)

Mobile Read (**www.mobileread.com**)

And also be sure to verify that the advice you are reading is specific to the 2020 Fire, because most of the support pages for the earlier Kindle Fire models don't apply to the new Fire tablets.

11. FIRE ACCESSORIES

Another thing that makes the Fire so much fun to own is the huge selection of accessories for it. Some of them are must-have items, and some of them are nice-to-have items, but all of them make your experience of owning a Fire just a little bit better. To shop for accessories, start in the Kindle Store on Amazon.

Cases, Stands, Skins and Screen Protectors

A nice case for your Fire is one of the first things you should buy after you purchase the device itself. We prefer a folio-style case that feels like a book when you hold it in your hands. Remember that the case should specifically say that it fits the new Fire HD, because cases for the Kindle Fires are not interchangeable. Look for a microfiber lining and a secure closure for the case cover so it doesn't accidentally come open. Another good feature is a set of grooves so you can use the case as a stand to make watching videos more comfortable. Be sure to pick a case that doesn't muffle the speakers on the rear of the Fire. Don't forget to pick out a color and fabric you like. Leather cases cost a bit more, but they do look sharp!

If you choose a case that doesn't double as a stand, you can buy a separate stand for video watching. Stands come in a number of designs, including folding travel stands, rigid stands, and stands with adjustable angles.

Lately skins have become all the rage for personalizing your smartphones and tablets. They are essentially a kind of sticker that you attach to your Fire - usually an easy enough process provided you follow the directions that come with the skins. You can buy all kinds of different skin designs for your Fire and there are even websites offering design-your-own custom skins. Make sure that any skin you purchase is compatible with your Fire's specs, and please be aware that these skins are purely decorative and do not provide any protective function at all!

The Kindle Store also sells several types of touchscreen covers for the Fire. You can buy inexpensive adhesive plastic film, or a more substantial anti-glare cover to fit over the screen. A good screen protector will keep your Fire's touchscreen from getting scratched without blocking your touch commands.

A quick search of the Amazon Kindle Store will turn up some nice stylus touch pens to make your swiping and tapping easier. People with big fingers will be especially happy with these! Now that we have a stylus, we use it all the time.

Car Seat Tablet Holders and Mounts

An item which may be of interest to parents, are the different tablet holders designed to attach to the driver or front passenger seats to hold a tablet so that passengers on the back seats can watch whatever you've downloaded onto it. Essentially, it is a clever alternative if your car doesn't have a built-in DVD player and seat screen system - and for some parents it is a lifesaver for those long holiday road trips! In a similar vein, you can also purchase tablet mounts that attach your tablet to the front dashboard area - useful to operate GPS systems or view a pre-downloaded map. With either of these items, double check that they fit the specs of both your car and your new Fire!

Chargers and Adapters

Amazon took the hint from numerous user reviews after the release of the 2012 Kindle Fire HD, which didn't include a charger. The new Fire tablets ship with a 9W adapter to use as a charging device along with a standard USB cable. The adapter charges the Fire in less than 4 hours from 0% to 100% by plugging it into a wall outlet and connecting it to your Fire with the USB cable. The adapter can provide your tablet with continuous AC power, but we have found that it's not very convenient to use our Fire with it tethered to a wall plug!

Another handy power source to have on hand is a car charger that plugs into your vehicle's 12-volt power supply. These often come bundled in a kit with a case and other accessories.

External Devices

The Fire packs a lot of hardware value into its small size, but you can make it even more valuable by plugging in an external device. We list some of the most popular ones below.

Fire Keyboard: There isn't a specific keyboard made by Amazon for any of their fire tablets. However there are plenty of 3rd party Bluetooth keyboards that you can use with the Fire HD 8 or HD 10. Start your search here - **www.amzn.to/3a8bKfz**

Headphones: Although the Fire's built-in speakers sound pretty good, a pair of high-end headphones can deliver sound quality good enough to satisfy music lovers, and even a cheap pair of earbuds will keep you from distracting the people around you when you're listening to music or watching videos. The headphone jack is located on the same edge as the power switch of your Fire.

Bluetooth Devices: The Fire's Bluetooth capability allows it to connect wirelessly to a number of external Bluetooth devices. You can purchase headphones, earpieces, microphones, headsets, and external keyboards with Bluetooth capability. These devices will turn your Kindle into something very much like a desktop computer, without a jumble of messy cords and cables.

To set up a Bluetooth connection between your Fire and a wireless device, called "pairing," you need to turn on the external device first and make sure it is within range. Consult your owner's manual for the external device and find out how to set it to pairing mode. Next, pick up your Fire and swipe down from the top of the screen to open the *Quick Actions Menu*. Tap the *Wireless icon* and then tap *Bluetooth*. Tap the *On* button next to enable Bluetooth. Look at the *Available Devices menu* to see if the Fire has detected the Bluetooth signal from the external device. Tap the device name to connect it to your Fire. There might be additional prompts or pairing instructions before the two devices can start "talking" to each other.

The Status Bar at the top of your screen will show the "B" Bluetooth icon when Bluetooth is turned on. Remember that turning off Bluetooth will extend the length of time between battery charges on your Fire.

And Finally...

So there you are, you should now have all the tips, tricks and user information you need to get the most out of your new Fire tablet.

We are confident that we have covered all the information you could need, but we are only human so if you think we have missed anything important, or could have explained something better, we would love to hear from you.

In fact we'd love to hear any comments you have about our book - you can contact us here: **BestKindleApps@gmail.com**

All feedback will be treated in strictest confidence and we will be more than happy to make improvements for our next edition where we can.

Just before we go we would like to ask for your help. As we're sure you know, book reviews on Amazon play a huge part in helping people choose what they should be reading - and it's one of the ways that small independent publishers, like us, can get our voices heard.

So if you've found this book helpful we'd love it if you could take a minute to leave us a review. Thank you for reading.